For the Glory of Their Game

Stories of Life in the NFL by the Men Who Lived It

Richard Whittingham

TRIUMPH
B O O K S
CHICAGO

Library of Congress Cataloging-in-Publication Data

Whittingham, Richard, 1939–2005
    For the glory of their game: stories of life in the NFL by the men who lived it /
[compiled by] Richard Whittingham.
      p. cm.
    Includes bibliographical references (p.) and index.
    ISBN 1-57243-607-7
      1. Football—United States—History. 2. Football players—United States—Anecdotes.
    3. National Football League. I. Title.

    GV954.W46 2004
    796.332'64'0973—dc22

                                 2004046040

This book is available in quantity at special discounts for your group or organization.
For further information, contact:

Triumph Books
542 South Dearborn Street
Suite 750
Chicago, Illinois 60605
(312) 939-3330
Fax (312) 663-3557

Printed in U.S.A.
ISBN-13: 978-1-57243-607-7
ISBN-10: 1-57243-607-7
Design by Eileen Wagner, Wagner/Donovan Design
All photos are courtesy of Vernon Biever unless indicated otherwise.

Contents

Foreword

I came to the National Football League in 1957, before the sport was the big business it is today—when it was a game you played because you flat-out loved it.

I was the bonus choice of the 1957 NFL draft (the first player selected), picked by the Packers, who were coming off a last-place, 4–8 season. But they didn't know what to do with me. Our coach during my first year, Lisle Blackbourn, tried me at quarterback, at halfback, at fullback, and all but gave up on me. The following year it was the same thing with Scooter McLean, who had replaced Blackbourn.

Those were two truly frustrating—not to mention losing—seasons, and included the single worst record in Green Bay history (1–10–1, in 1958). I was ready to quit pro football altogether and go back home to Kentucky. I didn't need the Packers, and they didn't seem to need me. I didn't want to be playing up there with a bunch of guys who didn't give a crap.

Then, in 1959, Vince Lombardi came to Green Bay. It was a turning point in my life and certainly in the Packers' story—and the NFL's, for that matter.

Lombardi got our attention immediately. From day one at Green Bay, we learned that things would never be the same. He told us if we didn't give him 100 percent all the time, our butts would be out of Green Bay. He laid down his rules right away.

That's what all of us needed. That's what I needed. From high school through college, I had coaches who bitched at me. That never bothered me. Lombardi bitched at everyone. He was tough—tougher than any coach I had ever known. But when he talked to us, he was direct and firm, and I started to want to play the game again.

He told me that I was going to be his halfback—not quarterback or fullback, but halfback. I had one position to focus on, and I was determined to make the best of it.

For eight years Vince Lombardi was the most important man in my life. I respected him as a coach, a leader, and, more importantly, as a friend. If I needed advice, I could talk to him. He was tougher on me than he was on most of the other players, but I needed that extra push.

It was a wonderful ride, those years that followed. The first year under Lombardi we went from having won only one game the year before to a 7–5–0 record. The next year we went to the NFL championship game, but lost to the Eagles. Then we took the NFL title two years in a row. We won another world championship in 1965, and the following year still another when we beat Kansas City in Super Bowl I.

It was a time in my life that I will treasure forever.

—*Paul Hornung*

Introduction

Mike Ditka, the player who defined the position of tight end in the sixties and who later went on to coach the Chicago Bears to a Super Bowl championship, summed it up succinctly and perceptively when he talked about his playing days in the National Football League: "We played for the love of the game." Paul Hornung, the Green Bay Packers' great halfback of the same era, corroborated it: "[We played] before the sport was the big business it is today—when it was a game you played because you flat-out loved it."

And indeed that was the way they played the game. There were no astronomical salaries in professional football, as there are today. Players in the postwar years of the forties, fifties, and most of the sixties had to work at off-season jobs in order to earn enough to see themselves comfortably through the year. And all the way into the eighties, all but a few players had to count on careers *after* their playing days to provide for their families and support a decent lifestyle; no one dreamed of making so much money during their NFL careers that they would never have to work again after they finally hung up their cleats.

Things changed drastically in professional football during the years following World War II and before the advent of television coverage in the late fifties. The 60-minute men—some All-Pro on both sides, offense and defense, like Chuck Bednarik and George Connor—gave way to the platoon system. Player place-kickers, like tackle Lou Groza and end Pat Summerall, were replaced by specialists who kicked like soccer players. Veterans and rookies alike showed up at training camp out of shape, desperately in need of conditioning if they were to make it through another grueling season of NFL football.

It was also an age when most players remained with the teams that drafted them; a player whose career was spent in two or three different NFL cities was somewhat of an anomaly in those days before free agency: Otto Graham was a Cleveland Brown, Ray Nitschke a Green Bay Packer, Roger Staubach a Dallas Cowboy, Walter Payton a Chicago Bear. Jersey No. 34 didn't have a different body in it every year or two.

The players were a raucous group, for the most part, as uninhibited off the field as they were savage on it. They loved the game, no doubt about it; they loved the fellowship and the camaraderie of being on a team with others whose goals were the same as theirs. It was intense, but it was—above all—fun.

And who can describe what it was like better than those who were there, the players who made the game what it is and entertained us all so well by doing it? That's what is in the pages that follow—the stories, anecdotes, and behind-the-scenes insights best told by those who were there, the players themselves. Let them tell you what a recruiting visit from Bear Bryant was like. Let Staubach confide the first thing he learned when he arrived at Navy. Let Jim Brown tell what the racial situation was like when he enrolled at Syracuse. Let the players describe the eyebrow-raising, under-the-table offers made to Tony Dorsett and Earl Campbell. Listen to Alex Karras talk about Big Daddy Lipscomb. Read what would-be tacklers thought about the dazzle of Gale Sayers and what running backs had to say about the painful encounters with Dick Butkus and Jack Lambert. There are revelations about the off-field behavior of Bobby Layne, the bravado of Joe Namath, and the out-and-out meanness of Conrad Dobler. There is the sad tale of the illness and death of Brian

Piccolo, offset by the hilarious reminiscences of Art Donovan and the outrageous observations of Hollywood Henderson.

They treat us to their own behind-the-scenes observations: Doug Flutie remembers *the Pass*, Bart Starr gives his view of the "Ice Bowl," Terry Bradshaw talks about triumphing at four different Super Bowls, Don Meredith shares his unique take on various things football-related. The great cast of characters in the drama of professional football—those who played it for the love of the game—have a lot to say, and *For the Glory of Their Game* is their forum.

As Frank Gifford once observed, "Pro football is like nuclear warfare. There are no winners—only survivors." And those survivors entertain us with their stories and remembrances in the pages that follow.

Hall of Famer Paul Hornung dives into the end zone for a Packers touchdown. The 176 points he scored in 1960 still stand as the most ever tallied in a single season by an NFL player (15 touchdowns, 15 field goals, and 41 extra points).

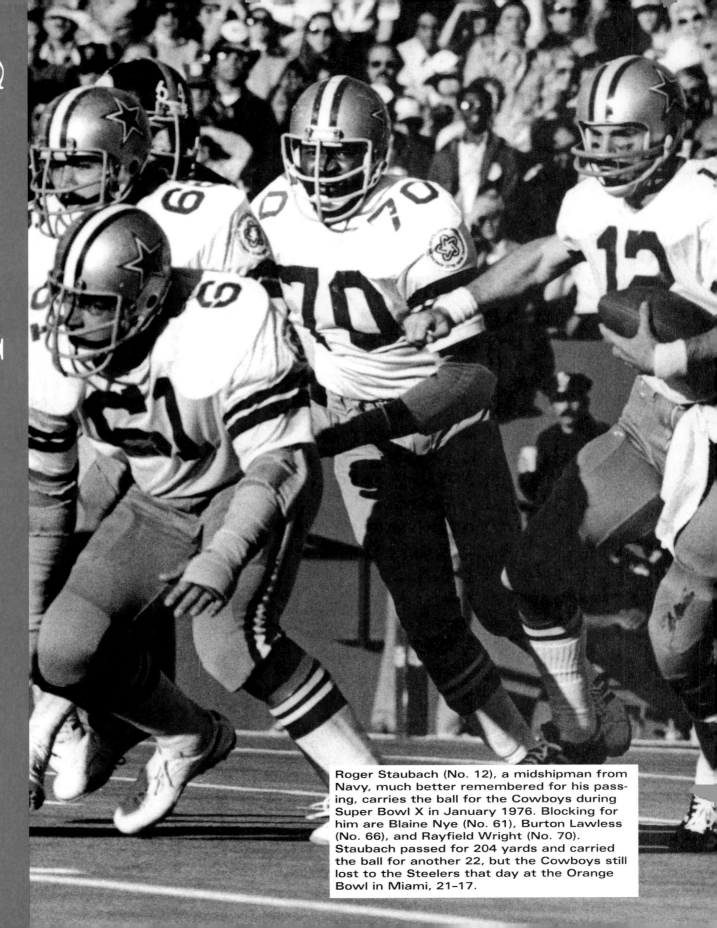

Section I

Roger Staubach (No. 12), a midshipman from Navy, much better remembered for his passing, carries the ball for the Cowboys during Super Bowl X in January 1976. Blocking for him are Blaine Nye (No. 61), Burton Lawless (No. 66), and Rayfield Wright (No. 70). Staubach passed for 204 yards and carried the ball for another 22, but the Cowboys still lost to the Steelers that day at the Orange Bowl in Miami, 21–17.

Getting Started

> "Football was fun. I was always higher on the field than any glow alcohol could ever produce."
>
> —KEN STABLER

Those who make it to the level of big-time college football, much less the National Football League, are a special breed of athlete indeed. Most of them say that football came into their lives very early, and from the very beginning it was a passion. From backyards and sandlots, to Pop Warner Leagues and high school, they harbored a dream. They strove with intense dedication to one day play in stadiums where tens of thousands of screaming fans would cheer them on or let them know with no reservation that they were the enemy.

The reminiscences of the great players here offer an insight into how it began for them, how they developed, and the quirks they encountered along the way. The first giant step has always been to the college level, separating, as they say, the men from the boys, the serious from the hobbyist. College recruiting has always been a daunting task for the recruiters and often a frightening and confusing situation for the recruits. But it is an integral part of the game of football in America, and hopeful stars of tomorrow have, for several generations, been thrilled or disappointed with college football scholarship offers (or the lack thereof). That's the way it's been, in fact, from the time when the helmets were soft and the grass was real, in the early days of the 20th century, to the world of paid scouts and computerized statistical analyses and assessments that are part of the 21st century recruiting process.

The ascent from major (and sometimes minor) college football to the ranks of the professionals is another enormous step that only a select few are able to take. The National Football League, since its birth in Canton, Ohio, in 1920, has been the ultimate goal of the best football players that America has to offer. The only way to get into the fraternity of professional football, however, is through the draft or perhaps in rare instances as a free-agent walk-on. Once in it, however, players find that it is a world unto itself.

In this section, we are taken from Ouachita Baptist College in Arkadelphia, Arkansas, to the Dallas Cowboys with Cliff Harris; we hear Ken Stabler's views on the legendary Bear Bryant; and share Jim Brown's memories of confrontation of the color barrier. There is a 15-year-old Rosey Brown at Morgan State University, a street-tough New York kid named Lyle Alzado exiled to Yankton College in South Dakota, a multitalented Bo Jackson trying to choose between Alabama and Auburn Universities, and a brash Jim McMahon encountering the Mormons of Brigham Young University in Utah. And there are the boys that came from football's cradle of greats in the mill towns of Pennsylvania: like Ditka, Marino, Unitas, Blanda, Buffone, and many others.

Their stories of getting started are as revealing as they are entertaining.

ROGER STAUBACH

As a boy in Cincinnati I followed college football. Especially Ohio State and Notre Dame. I had my heroes: Hopalong Cassady at Ohio State, Johnny Lujack and Johnny Lattner at Notre Dame, Pete Dawkins at Army, Joe Bellino at Navy. I dreamed of playing in college myself, and the dream came true. . . .

I was recruited by a number of teams—Ohio State, Purdue, Michigan—but the one that most caught my attention was Navy, and that came about by accident. One of their assistant coaches, Rick Forzano, had come to our school to take a look at our center and cocaptain, Jerry Momper. While he was watching film on Momper he noticed me and said he'd like to talk to me as well. He gave me the recruitment pitch and ended it with a smile and a shrug, saying, "We can't promise you anything other than that when you graduate, you can have your own battleship."

At Navy I learned fairly quickly that I could compete at the college level, but I learned the primary objective even faster. Literally, on the first day, after they clip your hair down to the scalp, you learn how to say, "Beat Army."

JIM BROWN

I went to Syracuse believing I was on scholarship, when actually I was there on a trial basis. It wasn't until after I graduated that Kenny [Molloy] explained his actions. He didn't want me to feel indebted, wanted me to think I had gotten into college entirely on my own. He felt Syracuse, with its proximity and blend of academics and sports, would be excellent for me. He'd been treated well at Syracuse, thought that I would be too. He didn't know because they didn't tell him: Syracuse did not want black athletes.

I was the only black on the freshman team and the only player living at Skytop [apartments]. All my freshman teammates lived in a dorm called Collendale, in the heart of campus. I was so naïve, I never even thought about race. I thought it was strange, left it at that.

My next discovery was also puzzling. All my teammates were given meal tickets that entitled them to eat at Slocum Hall. I was a big kid, always hungry, but my meal ticket was different—I was not to eat at Slocum, but at Sims, and my ticket provided for about half as much food. I decided to take matters into my own hands and the hands of a buddy: we started printing phony meal tickets. Terrified, we'd walk through the food line with our doctored tickets. Never got busted, though, and our stomachs got full.

DON MEREDITH

I was born in Mount Vernon, county seat of Franklin County, second smallest county in the great and sovereign state of Texas. [The] population was 1,423, as I remember. It was about 100 miles from Dallas.

We'd get the *Dallas Morning News*, and I was always reading about SMU [Southern Methodist University]. I did belong to the Methodist church, but I don't think that had anything to do with my going there. I knew they played in the Cotton Bowl and that was something, to me, anyway. I was a member of the 4-H Club, and we'd go up to the state fair and I'd look in at that Cotton Bowl and I'd think, "One of these days, I'd love to play football in the Cotton Bowl."

Another thing: while I was growing up there, I'd heard about Doak Walker and Kyle Rote and read about them when they were playing for SMU, and it was a dream of mine to follow them there and to play in the Cotton Bowl. I'd been courted by the University of Texas, and my older brother got a scholarship to TCU [Texas Christian University], but all along I wanted SMU and the Cotton Bowl.

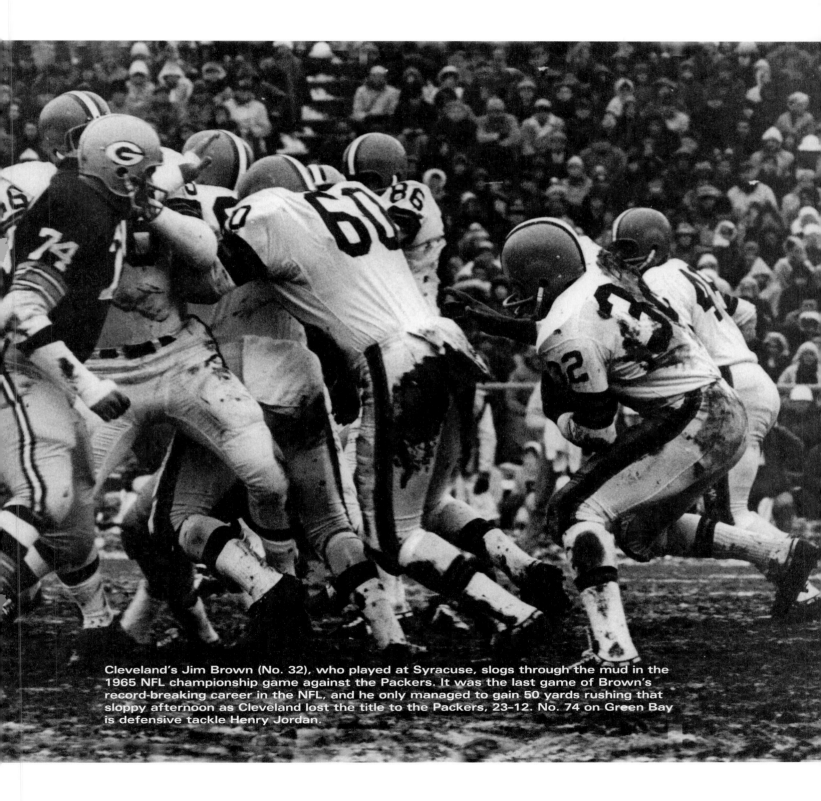

Cleveland's Jim Brown (No. 32), who played at Syracuse, slogs through the mud in the 1965 NFL championship game against the Packers. It was the last game of Brown's record-breaking career in the NFL, and he only managed to gain 50 yards rushing that sloppy afternoon as Cleveland lost the title to the Packers, 23–12. No. 74 on Green Bay is defensive tackle Henry Jordan.

"Dandy" Don Meredith (No. 17) hands off to Dallas fullback Don Perkins in a game in the midsixties. Meredith, who played college ball at Southern Methodist, was with the Cowboys from their very first year, 1960, and quarterbacked them through the 1968 season. In his nine-year career, he had a quarterback rating of 74.8, completing 1,170 of 2,308 passes (50.7 percent) for 17,199 yards and 135 touchdowns.

"When you're playing for the national championship, it's not a matter of life and death. It's more important than that."

—DUFFY DAUGHERTY

JIM MCMAHON

I was about 10 years old when I first started to play organized football. We had a Little League program out in San Jose, California. I remember the first day of practice: the coach had everybody line up, and whoever threw the football the farthest was the quarterback. I threw it the farthest, and that's how I became a quarterback.

After two years of high school ball in California, my family moved to Roy, Utah, and I finished up playing the last two years there. . . .

I wanted to play baseball in college, too, and Brigham Young had a good baseball program. That and the fact that it was close to home where my parents could . . . watch me play were the biggest reasons I went to BYU.

BYU wasn't what I thought college life was going to be like. If you're not a Mormon there, you hardly exist. . . . I knew a lot of people who went there and didn't stay more than a year. They just couldn't handle the constant pressure of the religion thing: every class began with a prayer, and you had to take 14 credit hours of the Mormon religion. And there weren't a whole lot of things a guy could do for social life if he didn't believe in what they believe in. . . .

Our head coach was LaVell Edwards, who had been there since 1972 and became one of the winningest coaches in college football. I got along with him all right, although there were times when we had our differences. There were people there who were always saying something that got back to him—it seemed every

Bears quarterback Jim McMahon (No. 9), who led Brigham Young during his college days, fakes to his right before handing off to fullback Calvin Thomas (No. 33) in a game against the Packers in the mideighties. McMahon quarterbacked the Bears to Super Bowl XX, where they captured the 1985 NFL championship, and to the playoffs in 1984, 1986, 1987, and 1988. Injuries plagued McMahon's otherwise fine career in Chicago (1982–1988) and brought it to a premature end.

Monday that I came back to school, somebody had said I was at a party somewhere in Roy or Provo, here or there, or I did this or that. The majority of it wasn't true.

At BYU all the plays were sent in from the sideline, but I had a lot of freedom to change plays there, and I did it quite often. We did have a great offensive system out there under Edwards, and we became known for it, but in the early years our football program didn't really get much respect because they didn't consider our conference [Western Athletic Conference] all that good—which I think was ridiculous. In my first two years there, Arizona and Arizona State were in our conference before they moved to the PAC-10. It wasn't until 1984, when BYU won the NCAA national championship, that the program got the recognition it deserved, [and] I contend the BYU team that won the NCAA title in 1984 couldn't have touched some of the teams we had when I was there [1977–1981].

> "Every time you make a football player think,
> you're handicappin' him."
>
> —BUM PHILLIPS

EARL CAMPBELL

I was offered scholarships from colleges all over the country. It was a remarkable time in my life. Coaches would travel all the way to Tyler, [Texas], to visit with my mother and me, trying to sell us on their schools and their football programs.

One thing I made perfectly clear to each of those recruiters was that Earl Campbell was not for sale. I was not going to be bought. Black people had been bought and sold for many years, and I was not going to continue that tradition. Some recruiters tried offering me cars and apartments. I wasn't interested. My college selection would be based only on academic and football programs. Plus, no one was going to drag this country boy out of Texas, so that narrowed down the list considerably. . . .

I made my final decision the day Texas Longhorns head football coach Darrell Royal showed up on my doorstep. It was an easy decision to make. Coach Royal walked into our home and seemed as comfortable with us as we were with him. I learned later that he had grown up very poor in Oklahoma during the dust bowl era, and then I understood why he felt right at home in our house. . . .

The day I signed that letter of intent was the first day of my new life. I would no longer be just another one of the Campbell boys. I would no longer be a country boy who worked in the rose fields, hauled hay, played pool, and strolled through town without attracting much notice. I was headed for the "bright lights," as my mother used to say.

GARY FENCIK

When I went off to college, playing pro football was never one of my considerations. I didn't think I was large enough. But I had a pretty good career at Yale, and in my senior year, when the scouts started sending stuff, I got my hopes up about being drafted.

In college, ironically, the two most memorable games I played in we lost. Both were against Harvard. In my junior year [1974], we went up to Cambridge, and they had Pat McInally, a wide receiver then, who later became quite a punter for the Cincinnati Bengals. We were undefeated and were winning, but they came back on a long drive and won it in the last few minutes. I had had a really good day—11 catches for something like 180 yards. [Better known as a free safety later with the Chicago Bears, Fencik was a wide receiver in college.] In my senior year we had

Houston Oilers running back Earl Campbell breaks free from New England's Rod Shoate during an AFC divisional playoff game in Foxboro, Massachusetts, on January 1, 1978. *Photo courtesy of AP/Wide World Photos.*

Chicago safety Gary Fencik, an Eli from Yale, hangs onto an interception in a game against the Packers in the Bears' championship season of 1985. Fencik's 38 interceptions during his 12-year NFL career in Chicago (1976–1987) remain the most in Bears history. No. 50 is Bears Hall of Fame middle linebacker Mike Singletary. *Photo courtesy of AP/Wide World Photos.*

another excellent team, but [Harvard] again beat us on a field goal in the last minute of the game.

Ivy League football was different. I remember Buddy Ryan, our defensive coach with the Bears, telling me on the plane coming back from an away game that he wanted me to go over and explain to Mike Singletary how difficult spring football was in the Ivy League. So I did. I told him [that] the first day we come out and work out, and the scouts are there. At the end of the day we have a barbecue, which is fairly traditional at Yale, and after it Carm Cozza [Yale's longtime head coach] says, "We'll see you boys next fall." We were allowed only one day of spring practice in the Ivy League.

BO JACKSON

Alabama didn't send a plane for me. Tuscaloosa was too close. In Alabama, that was almost like getting a call from God. I was a "Roll, Tide!" fan myself; they were the national champions when I was in high school. I went over to Tuscaloosa on a Saturday and met Bear Bryant and went up in his famous tower with him while the Tide was practicing.

"Bo, we'd love to have you here," he said in his raspy voice. "We think you could help us in a lot of ways. Offense or defense."

Defense? Right away, I became less of an Alabama fan. The way I figured it, if I went there, they were going to make me into a linebacker. I didn't want that. I wanted to run with the ball.

Ken Donahue, the coach who was recruiting me for Alabama, told me that as a running back, I probably wouldn't play at all my freshman year and maybe just a little my sophomore year. . . .

The more I heard, the less I liked the idea of going to Alabama. I visited Auburn, and I liked what Pat Dye, their new coach, said to me. "If you come to Auburn," he said, "I'm not gonna give you anything. You got to earn it. Don't expect to be put up on a pedestal. You've got to work your ass off. But if you do, the accolades will come, the pros will look at you, and you will be compensated. The one thing Auburn can give you is a good education."

FRANK GIFFORD

It had been a great experience at USC [University of Southern California]. My coach at Bakersfield High School, a man by the name of Homer Beattie, had played for USC, and at that time, he was certainly one of the most important persons in my life. He got me going in the right direction academically as well as on the football field. I hadn't been one of the greatest students. He felt I could possibly play for USC, and he knew I would have to qualify on both levels if I were to be accepted at that school.

After my fourth year at Bakersfield, USC did indeed offer me a football scholarship, but I was deficient in a few academic units and I had to make them up. So I went for a year to Bakersfield Junior College, and then moved on to USC.

At USC, they never really could find just what to do with me. I had played offense and defense in high school and ended up a T-formation quarterback my junior year. I played safety on defense. And in my senior year, they switched to a wing-T, and I became a running back. Then in junior college, we had an offense where I both ran and passed the ball.

So, at USC, I didn't exactly fit anywhere in particular. For two years, I played defense. Then, in my senior year, they brought in a new coach, Jess Hill, and he designed an offense that was pretty much suited to me—a single wing and a wing-T—

Bo Jackson, the two-sport star and running back for the Los Angeles Raiders, takes off on a 45-yard run against the Kansas City Chiefs during the fourth quarter of a 1989 game at the Los Angeles Coliseum. *Photo courtesy of AP/Wide World Photos.*

New York Giant Frank Gifford (No. 16), a threat running with the ball, passing it, or catching it, rolls out and looks for a receiver here in a game against the Colts in the fifties. Gifford, who earlier starred for Southern Cal, played in five NFL championship games during his 12-year career with the Giants and was selected for seven Pro Bowl appearances. No. 79 is tackle Rosey Brown.

and I was sort of the focus of it, running and passing and receiving. He also had a fine staff with Mel Hein and Don Clark, who would later become head coach at Southern Cal. And it made a big difference. We were 2–5–2 in 1950, my junior year, and won our first seven games in 1951. The fifth game that we won that year was over the University of California, and at the time they were ranked number one in the nation and had a 39-game winning streak. Well, after that all the bells went off and we jumped from nothing to something like fourth or fifth in the nation. Suddenly the press and the media were all over the campus, and a week later I was being photographed for All-American. It was the weirdest thing—we all kept wondering how it happened so fast.

We didn't go to the Rose Bowl because we lost our last three games that year, but I did play in the East-West game and the Senior Bowl.

"There were only three men in the whole world
I was ever afraid of: my old man, Bear Bryant,
and George Halas."

—George Blanda

JOE NAMATH

When I was a high school senior, a coach from the University of Michigan came to talk to me about college. Somebody told him he could find me at the Blue Room. When he got there, I was out front, lying on the hood of a car. He didn't even bother to talk to me. I guess he decided I wasn't the University of Michigan type.

The irrepressible Joe Namath looked intent during Super Bowl III. Namath, who fine-tuned his trade under Bear Bryant at Alabama, led the underdog Jets that January day in 1969 to the AFL's first world championship, defeating the Baltimore Colts, 16–7. Three days before the game, Namath announced, "I'll guarantee [a victory]" over the three-touchdown-favored Colts.

Dan Hampton (No. 99), who played both defensive end and defensive tackle for the Bears, has his sights set on interrupting this Packers play during the eighties. The Bears-Packers rivalry is one of the longest—and perhaps the most storied—in NFL history, dating back to 1921. Hampton, an All-American from the University of Arkansas, played 12 years with the Bears, went to four Pro Bowls, was named to the Pro Football Hall of Fame's All-Star Team of the eighties, and holds an unofficial record of 11 knee surgeries from injuries while playing in the NFL.

DAN HAMPTON

When I was a kid, the doctor told me I'd never play football again. I was in the sixth grade, and I fell 45 feet out of a tree. I crushed my right heel and broke my legs in three or four places. I was in a wheelchair with a hip cast on my legs for six months. The doctor said I'd never walk comfortably, let alone run.

Then, when I was a junior in high school, some of the coaches and players talked me into coming out for the team. I was rusty, and it took a while to kind of get in the groove. . . . I [also] had bad eyes in high school. I used to squint all the time. One day the coaches got on me about some kind of tackling technique thing. I remember, I said, "Well, Coach, quite honestly, I can't really tell if he's got the ball. I can't see that good." He asked me how the hell I could tackle anybody then. So, I said, "Well, I just tackle everybody, and the one that strugglers the hardest, I know he's the one with the ball." I got contact lenses when I went to Arkansas.

I had scholarship offers from a lot of places, but the only place I wanted to go was Arkansas. My dad had been a Razorback fan, and he had died when I was in the eighth grade, so it was kind of something I thought he would really have wanted me to do. So I went up to Fayetteville, and things worked out, and by my senior year, I was rocking and rolling pretty good.

KEN STABLER

Southeast Conference colleges had begun recruiting me my junior year [1964], and an Alabama alumnus got me a job with a local lumber company. I drove a forklift truck in the yard and also made deliveries to construction sites. It put some cash in my pocket.

The recruiting intensified my senior year as we again went undefeated and won the Gulf Shores football championship. I was named to the all-state, all-southern, and

Ken Stabler, another quarterback who trained under Bear Bryant at Alabama, shown here during his two-year stopover with Houston (1980–1981), had his biggest impact as a quarterback with the Raiders from 1970 through 1979, leading them to Super Bowl XI, where they defeated the Vikings 32–14 for the 1976 NFL title. Stabler finished out his NFL career with New Orleans (1982–1984).

to two All-American teams. I was also named MVP in the annual postseason all-star game played by the top seniors in the state.

Auburn and Alabama alumni had each taken me to see their teams play, trying to convince me that their program would be best for me. The Auburn offense was closer to the style I was used to playing, with the quarterback running more than passing, and I was leaning toward that school. But Auburn wasn't winning, and Alabama always won. Alabama also had Paul W. Bryant Hall, probably the finest athletic dorm in the land.

But the greatest thing Alabama had to offer was Paul W. Bryant himself, the legendary "Bear."

When coach Bryant came down to Foley [Alabama] and had dinner with my family, he just filled our little dining room. He didn't make any sales pitches. He just talked about hunting and fishing in that deep, gravelly voice that all but hypnotized you.

I decided right then that if I was going to bust my ass playing college football, I was going to do it for the man they called "Bear."

RAY NITSCHKE

I was one of 33 high school players picked for an all-state football squad. I got to eat dinner at the executive mansion in Springfield, Illinois, with Governor William G. Stratton. All of us on the squad also went to Champaign-Urbana to hear a talk by the governor, but the speech I paid more attention to there was given by Ray Eliot. He was the Illinois coach and one of my heroes. We got to meet the entire Illinois squad. Pete Palmer, "the Illini's singing tackle," sang a new song called "Illinois" and introduced the homecoming queen, Margie Burger, and the nine coeds of her court, who gave us autographed pictures of themselves.

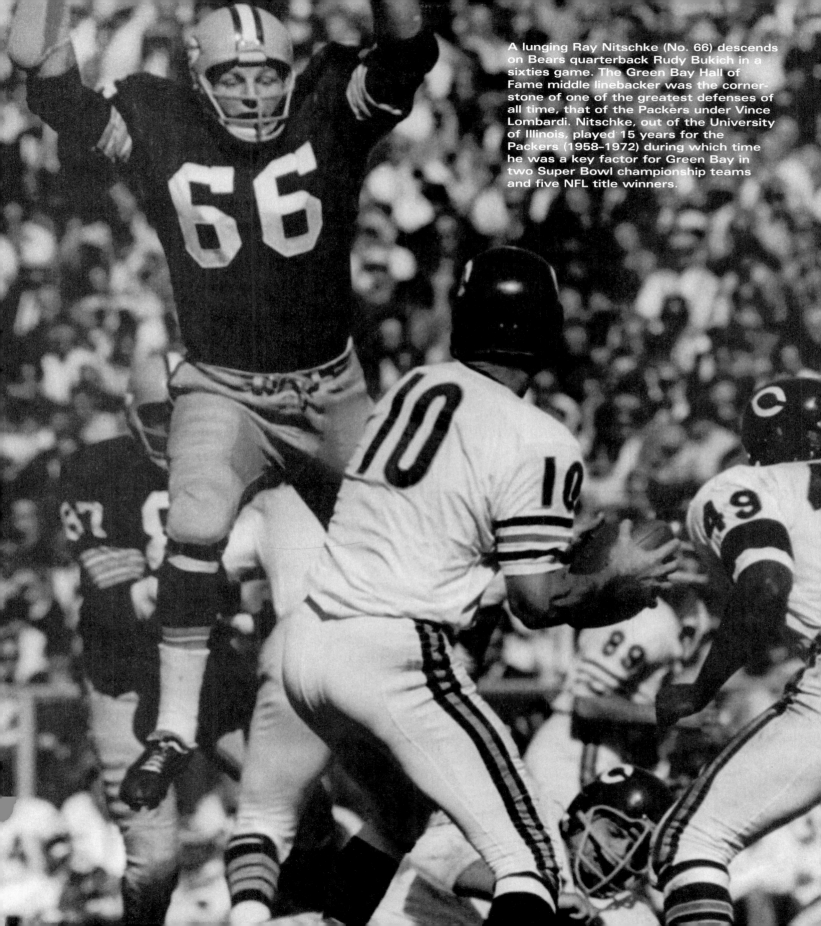

A lunging Ray Nitschke (No. 66) descends on Bears quarterback Rudy Bukich in a sixties game. The Green Bay Hall of Fame middle linebacker was the cornerstone of one of the greatest defenses of all time, that of the Packers under Vince Lombardi. Nitschke, out of the University of Illinois, played 15 years for the Packers (1958–1972) during which time he was a key factor for Green Bay in two Super Bowl championship teams and five NFL title winners.

[Major league baseball's] St. Louis Browns would give me $3,000 to just sign my name, and that seemed like all the money in the world. . . . Getting a chance to play in the big leagues appealed to me. I'd always enjoyed baseball. It's an individualist's game. Compared to football, it's easy. . . .

But Andy Puplis [Nitschke's high school football coach] said not to sign with the Browns: "Get yourself an education, Ray. Make something of yourself."

So I went to Illinois and played football and got myself an education.

ALEX WEBSTER

My first encounter with organized football was back in Kearny, New Jersey—which is just north of Newark—where I was born and raised. That's where I started playing the game in junior high school. . . .

I was lucky to have gotten a whole bunch of scholarship offers after finishing [high] school in Kearny. I took a couple of trips to see the colleges. I went over to Tennessee in Knoxville and down to the University of Miami [Florida] and a couple of other schools. Then I went to take a look at North Carolina State, which is in Raleigh—there's that whole complex of universities in the area there with North Carolina in Chapel Hill and Duke in Durham, all neighbors.

Well, I really liked that area of the country, and the university was very appealing. The coach there was Beattie Feathers, who had gone to Tennessee and later was a fine running back for the Chicago Bears. In fact, he was the first running back in the NFL to gain more than 1,000 yards rushing in a single season [1,004 in the 13-game season of 1934]. Of course, he had Bronko Nagurski blocking for him that year, which helped considerably.

Giants fullback Alex Webster (No. 29) drags along a Packers defender in the 1961 NFL championship game at City Stadium (now Lambeau Field) in Green Bay. Despite his valiant efforts, the Giants were swamped that day by Vince Lombardi's invincible Packers, 37–0. Initially snubbed by the NFL, Webster, from North Carolina State, played in the Canadian Football League (1953–1954) before joining the Giants. When he ended his 10-year career in New York he held most of the club's rushing records, including carries, yards gained, and touchdowns scored. No. 87 on Green Bay is defensive end Willie Davis.

There was a fellow by the name of Al Rotella, who was originally from New Jersey, but had gone to Tennessee and was now an assistant coach under Beattie at North Carolina State. In fact, all of Beattie's staff were former Tennessee ballplayers. It was Al Rotella who recruited me, got me to go down to the school, and introduced me to Beattie Feathers.

Well, Beattie had a wonderful heart, and he made me feel I had a good deal of potential in his system at North Carolina State. So I took their offer, and it was a good decision. My father had died when I was nine years old, and Beattie became just like a father to me. He and the whole coaching staff there were great.

North Carolina State was not a big school in those days, back in the early fifties. It was basically an engineering and agricultural school. And it was a place where I felt I would really have a chance to play. They were still playing the single wing, and that's what I had played in high school back in New Jersey. I'd been the tailback, and I also played free safety on defense. State was playing the old Tennessee system with the balanced line that General [Bob] Neyland had developed. It focused on running out of the single wing, and that was good for me because as a senior in high school, I had suffered a shoulder separation, and I wasn't throwing the football very well.

Running was what I wanted to do and what I did best.

I had a good four years down there in North Carolina. I played tailback and free safety, just like high school, and we did pretty well. That's where I got the nickname Big Red. I had red hair back then, and my face was always red because of the simple fact that I was fair-skinned and was out in the sun so much down there. I think my head looked like a big, red apple most of the time. Anyway, that old nickname has stuck through the years.

"Football is a nasty game, and you have
to be nasty to play it."

—Mike Ditka

THOMAS "HOLLYWOOD" HENDERSON

What I really wanted to do after high school was play football. Football had that winning combination of fun and notoriety. I had gotten a good taste of it, and I wanted some more. I was going to prove to my grandmother that I was going to play football, and it wasn't going to cost me any money to go to college. Besides, I had told all my friends in all the bars around Oklahoma City that I was going to play in the pros, so I started working on that again.

I just knew that Langston University, a small, black college 35 miles north of Oklahoma City, would take me. So I just showed up there, unannounced. I just walked on the field and went up to coach Albert Shoats and Roosevelt "Big Daddy" Nivens and told them I wanted to play football for them.

We went right inside the coach's office to talk. "I wanted to recruit you," coach Shoats told me, "you're a hell of a football player, but I thought Oklahoma was going to get you, or Oklahoma State."

"Yeah, everybody thought everybody else was going to get me, but here I am."

It was more likely that coach Shoats read the *Black Dispatch* more than Barry Switzer did. I didn't tell them that I'd never heard from Oklahoma State or Oklahoma, or that I couldn't make the body count at Wichita State.

"Well, we're glad to have you, son." Right then and there, he gave me a grant-in-aid and told me to move on campus.

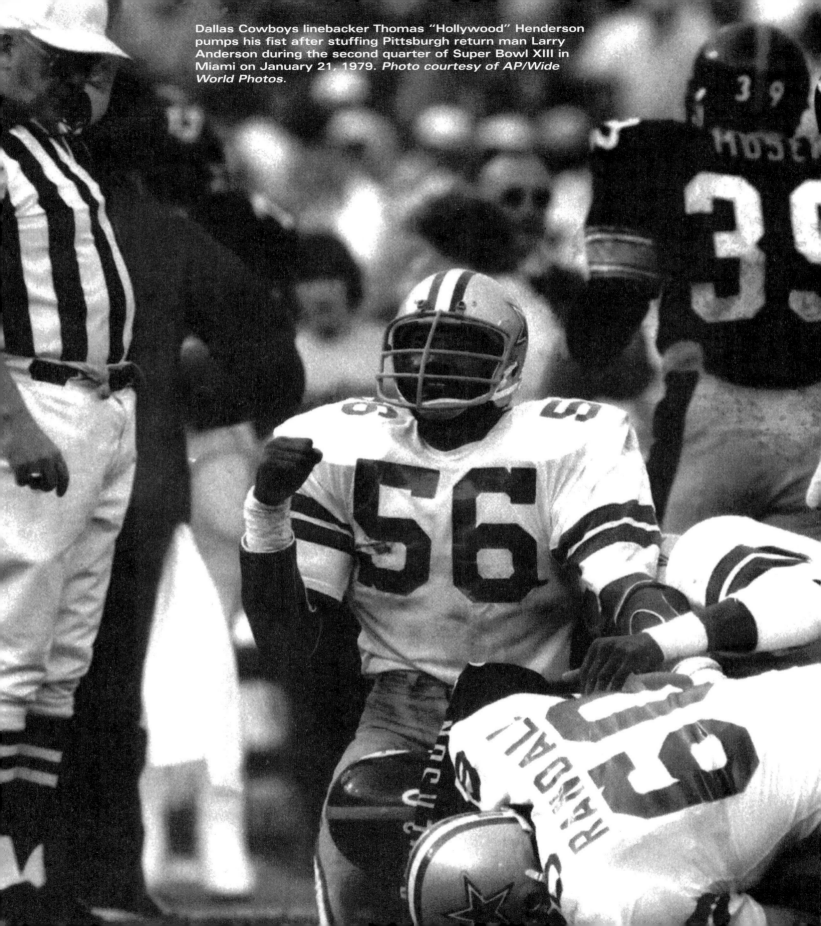

Dallas Cowboys linebacker Thomas "Hollywood" Henderson pumps his fist after stuffing Pittsburgh return man Larry Anderson during the second quarter of Super Bowl XIII in Miami on January 21, 1979. *Photo courtesy of AP/Wide World Photos.*

PAT SUMMERALL

I got into what you might call semiorganized football in junior high school down in Lake City, in northern Florida—the town where I was born and raised. It was in high school that I really got to love playing football. [But] I had had a rather unfortunate childhood. I was born with a clubfoot—the right one. Basically, it was turned around backward. At the time, the way they treated it was by breaking both bones in the bottom of the leg and just turning the foot around. The doctor told my mother afterward that I would be able to walk, but I would probably never be able to run or play with other kids. As time passed, however, through nature's help and the good Lord's help, it got better and better. As it turned out, that was the foot I used to kick with—although that was way down the road.

By the time I got to high school, things had pretty well worked out. I was on the track team and ran the 100-yard dash and the 440. I ran the 100 in about 10.1, which at that time was considered pretty good. I also played baseball and, of course, football. . . .

I went on a lot of college recruiting trips as a high school senior. In those days, you could go and put on a uniform and work out with the college teams, a lot of things like that. The NCAA rules have changed considerably since then. The two places that I was invited to, and was most serious about, were West Point and the University of Florida. West Point, I thought when I went there, looked a little too much like a jail. They were also suggesting that they would be sending me first to Kentucky Military Institute to study to be sure I could pass Army's entrance exams—my high school grades weren't all that good. Adding these things up, I decided I didn't really want to go there.

At the University of Florida, they wanted me to play both basketball and football. At that time it was relatively easy to do that because the seasons were shorter

Pat Summerall, an alumnus of the University of Arkansas, handled place-kicking duties for two teams, the Chicago Cardinals and the New York Giants, during his 10-year NFL career (1952–1961). Here he boots one for the Giants with Charlie Conerly holding. In the age before kickers were specialists, Summerall also played offensive and defensive end. He later, as all football fans know, went on to a long career as a television football broadcaster, teamed with John Madden to cover regular-season games and Super Bowls.

and the quality of both games was not nearly what it is today. Anyway, I didn't want to do that.

At the same time, my high school football coach, a gentleman named Hobart Hooser, had been hired by the University of Arkansas as their line coach. Well, he had been kind of like a father to me. He came back down to Florida and talked to me about going to Arkansas, and I went.

It was at Arkansas where I really got started as a kicker. When I was a sophomore—that must have been 1949—the coaching staff was not happy with the guy who was kicking off, not field goals or extra points. They said anyone who'd like to try kicking should come on out 30 minutes early this one day. "Well," I said, "what the heck, I'll give it a try." So I did. And it seemed to be something that was very natural to me. From then on, I kicked off for Arkansas.

DOUG BUFFONE

I came from western Pennsylvania, a town called Yatesboro. Coal mining. My dad was a coal miner; his brothers were all coal miners. It was a true coal-mining town: company houses were built by the coal-mining company; you had the company store. When I was 13 or 14, we moved to a house that had indoor plumbing and stuff like that. . . .

It is amazing, though, when you think that out of that little area, within a radius of about 50 miles there in western Pennsylvania, came so many great football players, guys like Mike Ditka, Jack Ham, Jim Kelly, Dan Marino, Terry Hanratty, Johnny Unitas, George Blanda. . . .

When I first started playing football, I was an offensive tackle and a linebacker. I played both ways in high school, and it was expected of you in college back then

Bears outside linebacker Doug Buffone, front-toothless here, played for Chicago from 1966 through 1979. Buffone was a center on offense at the University of Louisville. His 14-year NFL career is the longest (tied with Hall of Fame linebacker Bill George) in Bears history. He was defensive captain from 1972 through 1979. Hugging Buffone is defensive back Craig Clemons.

too. If you're from Pennsylvania and thinking of playing college ball, you think Penn State, Pitt, Notre Dame. Well, I tried all those schools. Scholastically, I could have gotten in—there was no problem—but I wasn't big. I was only 185 pounds, and they said, "You can't play tackle at 185." All three said, "The kid is just too small."

I kept looking, and finally I lucked out when the University of Louisville called. Louisville was not known at that time as a great powerhouse in football, but they said they'd give me and my brother scholarships. I played linebacker [at Louisville], and I also played offense for two or three years at center.

TONY DORSETT

A lot of head coaches came to Hopewell [Pennsylvania] to watch me. This was something new for the school, because until then only assistant coaches had come around. There was a lot of excitement when Frank Kush of Arizona State and Joe Paterno of Penn State visited Hopewell. But I think Woody Hayes of Ohio State made the biggest hit. It turned out he was a history buff, and he spent almost as much time talking history with the faculty as he did watching me play. . . .

I got some pretty incredible offers: X dollars for this, X dollars for that. Help do this for my family. Help do that for my girlfriend. I was saying, "Hey, wait a minute, man. How can you do all that for me? There's no way you can give me all those things." But it was serious talk: cars, homes, jobs for members of my family.

One very prominent college football coach—who, incidentally, is still prominent today—approached me with an envelope filled with money.

"This is what you want, kid," he said. "Take it. Come on, there's plenty more where this came from."

The Cowboys' great running back Tony Dorsett breaks through a gaping hole in the Packers defense in a game during the eighties. An All-American at the University of Pittsburgh before coming to the NFL, Dorsett earned star status in Dallas his rookie year, 1977, when he gained 1,007 yards rushing. He remained the Cowboys'—and one of the NFL's—premiere running backs throughout the eighties.

Baltimore Colts great Art Donovan runs onto the field for a 1962 ceremony in his honor following his retirement after the 1961 season. The five-time All-Pro defensive tackle played 12 seasons in the NFL and was inducted into the Pro Football Hall of Fame in 1968. *Photo courtesy of AP/Wide World Photos.*

ART DONOVAN

To be honest, Notre Dame may have come to the same realization I did regarding my presence there. The football coach, Frank Leahy, and I got off to a bad start almost immediately. During spring practice I thought I did fairly well. In fact, the guy who was going to be captain the following year, Pat Filley, told me one day that I was one of the only recruits kicking ass during scrimmages with the varsity. But I got into a fight with an offensive tackle during one of the first days of spring practice, and it turned out that the guy was one of Leahy's protégés. He was a big old tub of lard from New Orleans named Tiny Thorpe.

The guy had been holding me all practice. And I had warned him, "I don't like you as it is. Keep holding me and we're going to get into a fight." He did. And we did. Those things happen on the football field, and the incident itself didn't bother Leahy as much as the fact that I wouldn't shake hands with Tiny after they separated us. The guy was a jerk, and shaking hands with him wasn't going to make him any less of a jerk. But Leahy told me right in front of the whole team that he didn't like or need my type around there.

I still don't understand what Leahy's type was.

DOUG FLUTIE

When I got to Boston College I was probably about eighth on the depth chart. All these upperclassman were ahead of me, and within the first couple of weeks it became really frustrating.

I was about fourth-string on the depth chart by the end of training camp. The first-string quarterback, John Loughery, who was a junior, tore a ligament in his thumb, and the second- and third-string guys, Doug Guyer and Dennis Scala, who were also juniors, played the first three games. They couldn't do the job. We were getting blown out. John Loughery played the fourth game against Penn State, and he completed only one of fifteen passes for two yards. At halftime, Barry Gallup told me to loosen up because I might get a chance to play. I thought, yeah, right. Here we are at Penn State. There [are] eighty-five thousand fans in the seats. I just shook my head at Barry.

Around the start of the fourth quarter, they told me to start warming up. We were losing 38–0. I remember walking onto the field, with the sun shining brightly. I thought, this is something I could tell my kids or grandkids about some day. I figured it was probably a one-time shot, that I'd go out and mess around and play the last few series.

"Pro football is like nuclear warfare.
There are no winners—only survivors."
—FRANK GIFFORD

CLIFF HARRIS

I was a small kid, but I played football, and I remember in the 10th grade our coach saying to me, "Cliff, you're too small to play football. Why don't you go back and concentrate on your studies?" This was in Hot Springs, Arkansas, and then we moved to the little town of Desart, Arkansas, and I ignored the advice and played football there. I was the quarterback on our high school team.

My father had gone to Ouachita Baptist College, which is located in the foothills of the Ozarks in the town of Arkadelphia. It's a liberal arts college with maybe a thousand or so students. It's a beautiful campus surrounded by pine trees

Perennial All-Pro Cowboys safety Cliff Harris makes a diving stab to knock away a pass intended for St. Louis Cardinals receiver J. V. Cain in a 1976 game at Texas Stadium. Coming in from the right is safety Charlie Waters, and underneath is cornerback Mel Renfro (No. 20).

and on the banks of the Ouachita River. My father had played football there, and I followed.

The head coach was Buddy Bob Benson, and he taught us that we would win through mental toughness. So we had extraordinarily difficult practices—the practice field was down in a kind of bottomland and the humidity was always around 100 percent—and he would say, "If we don't have the talent to win, we will have the toughness to win."

Ouachita was an NAIA [National Association of Intercollegiate Athletics] division six school, and we played teams like Mississippi College and Austin College in Texas. I still played quarterback then. Then, in my junior year, one of the most exciting things happened in my entire college career—we earned the chance to play in the NAIA divisional playoff bowl. We rode on a bus for about 16 hours and played in what they called the Peanut Bowl in Dauphin Island, Alabama, against Livingston State. Before the game, they gave each of the players a bag of peanuts.

Two years later [1970], I was with the Dallas Cowboys, and we played in the Super Bowl [V]. A headline in one of the Arkansas newspapers was: From the Peanut Bowl to the Super Bowl!

TED ALBRECHT

I got my start playing football in the Pop Warner League in Vallejo, California; I was around 13 years old.

[In high school] they put down this plank that was 12 inches wide and eight feet long. There was a line drawn in the middle. You had to put your hand down at one end of the plank, and the opposing lineman did the same at the other end, the idea being that you meet full-speed at the four-foot mark and see who could drive the

40

Grizzled is the best way to describe Chicago Bears tackle Ted Albrecht in this photo. An All-American at Berkeley, Albrecht was a first-round draft pick by Chicago in 1977 and made the NFL's All-Rookie Team that year. A career-ending injury cut short his fine stint on the Bears offensive line in 1981.

other guy off the plank. I was a sophomore when I first did that, up against a senior who was an inch or two taller and maybe 40 pounds heavier, and he just creamed me. We had a terrific fullback and he grabbed me by the back of the helmet and dragged me up. "Do you see that fence down there?" It was about 50 yards away. "Well, that's what you run down the plank for, the fence; forget the plank, forget the guy in between." The next time I did it, I didn't stop, and I knocked the guy right off the board. I got the idea . . . just be violent as hell: just kick ass. It was my first real football lesson.

I was recruited by maybe a hundred schools. They didn't have all-state rankings in California, but I had a good reputation as a major lineman, and I had the size. I even got some letters from Big Ten schools, but I concentrated my 10 visits on schools in the PAC-8, as it was then known, and other western state schools. I visited Arizona, Arizona State, Washington, Oregon, UCLA, Stanford—all of them. But I selected Cal-Berkeley [University of California at Berkeley] because I knew it was a great institution, I thought Mike White was a wonderful coach, and I knew I really had a chance to play. UCLA recruited me, and they swore they weren't recruiting any junior college transfers. Pepper Rodgers was their coach, and they had something like 180 guys out for football the year I went to Cal-Berkeley, counting all the transfers and everybody else.

The offensive line coach at Cal my first year was Howard Mudd. He had been a wonderful offensive guard for the San Francisco 49ers in the sixties and had played his last two years in the NFL with the Bears [1969–1970]. When I first met him he said, "What I'm going to try to teach you in the next four years is that an offensive lineman is basically a bag of tricks. Inside that bag are all the tools you'll need to be the best in the business. Develop them. Use them. Set your ultimate football goal on becoming a professional when these four years are over."

The bag of tricks he was talking about included such things as concentrating on being mentally tough, how to position yourself, how to use leverage, and how to handle yourself so that you're never off balance. And if you have to hold, how to hold and when to hold. Of course, I *never* held.

ROSEY BROWN

I was born in Charlottesville, Virginia, and that's where I went to school. I played football in high school—offensive and defensive tackle—and after my senior year, the coach from Morgan State College in Baltimore came down and offered me a scholarship. My mother thought that was a fine thing, and she said that's where I would be going. In those days, the mothers made the decisions; nowadays it's more the kids who make the decisions.

So I went on up to Morgan State in 1949. I actually started college when I was 15, and I graduated when I was 19.

In those days, Morgan was an all-black school. And they had a very good football team then—I believe they had won something like 52 straight games by the time I arrived. We played against other all-black schools, like Virginia State College; Virginia Union [University]; Hampton College, which was also in Virginia; Howard University, in Washington, D.C.; and schools like that—mostly from that area.

One game I particularly remember from that time was against Central State College, which was in Wilberforce, Ohio. We both traveled to New York to play each other at the Polo Grounds. We were the first two black schools to play outside of our conference. That was my very first trip to New York.

Coming from Virginia to Baltimore was something, but nothing like coming to New York for the first time. The only way I can explain it is like I was starry-eyed, taking in something I'd never seen the likes of before.

Roosevelt "Rosey" Brown (No. 79) takes a breather on the Giants sideline. The Hall of Fame–bound tackle anchored the Giants' offensive line from 1953 through 1965. A 27th-round draft choice out of tiny Morgan State College in Baltimore who played in an all-black-school conference in Maryland, Brown went to nine Pro Bowls and was named All-Pro eight times during his illustrious 13-year Giants career.

44

Mike Ditka, one of the game's greatest tight ends, heads out for the Bears after gathering in a pass in a game against Green Bay in the sixties. An All-American from the University of Pittsburgh, Ditka was Chicago's first-round draft choice in 1961 and was also that year's NFL Rookie of the Year. After an outstanding six years with the Bears, he played two seasons with the Eagles (1967–1968) and four with the Cowboys (1969–1972). Pursuing him is Packers defensive back Hank Gremminger (No. 46).

MIKE DITKA

I wanted to go to Notre Dame all the time I was a kid. I always listened to Notre Dame on the radio, and being a Catholic, that was a great thing. I heard from Notre Dame, too. I heard from them first, and I never heard from them again. The first letter I got was from Jim Finks. He was an assistant coach under Terry Brennan, but he left Notre Dame and went to Canada. The next Notre Dame letter I got was from Bernie Crimmins. I went to visit, but it was summer and no one was there. I had already nailed it down to either Pitt or Penn State.

The guy who recruited me at Penn State was Joe Paterno, who was Rip Engle's top assistant. The guy at Pitt was Jack Wiley, who was John Michelosen's assistant. To this day, my parents wish I had gone to Penn State. They don't regret I went to Pitt, but they were really impressed with the Penn State people and program. Joe Paterno impressed them. But I wanted to be a dentist, and that entered into my decision. Pro ball was never a consideration at that time. Dentistry was the consideration. I remember talking to an athlete at Penn State who was an All-American in baseball. He said if I wanted to be a dentist, I should go to Pitt because it was easier to get into dental school there.

JIM KATCAVAGE

I'm a Philadelphia kid—born in Wilkes-Barre but moved to Philadelphia, where I've been ever since. I played football at Roman Catholic High School there. I also played on the basketball team. And that—the basketball—kind of changed where I ended up going to college.

In my senior year, I dislocated my shoulder playing basketball and had to have it operated on. A couple of the colleges who had expressed interest in giving me a

Jim Katcavage, who played his college ball at the University of Dayton, joined one of the NFL's all-time great defenses when he was drafted by the Giants in 1956. A defensive end, he was part of the game's original "Fearsome Foursome," complementing Andy Robustelli, Rosey Grier, and Dick Modzelewski. They fronted the New York defense in the late fifties and early sixties. Katcavage gained a starting berth on the Giants defensive line his rookie year and would not relinquish it until he retired 13 years later.

football scholarship—and ones where I would have liked to have gone—weren't interested anymore. When they learned about the shoulder and the operation, they just faded away. My high school football coach managed to wangle a scholarship for me to the University of Dayton in Ohio. It was a one-year scholarship based on my making the team. I did, and after that, they extended the scholarship for the following three years.

We played NCAA Division I then, but we did not play really big-time college football. In 1954, when I was a junior, though, we went down to play Tennessee; they had Johnny Majors as their tailback, and he was to become an All-American, and Tom "the Bomb" Tracy at fullback, who later played for a bunch of NFL teams. We were a big underdog, but we almost beat them—we lost 14–7.

Dayton was a small school in terms of football. We didn't get much publicity outside of the city itself. I was lucky, though. After I finished there, I was invited to the College All-Star Game in Chicago, which was in 1956. There were an awful lot of good football players on our team: Earl Morrall of Michigan State, Hopalong Cassady of Ohio State, Ron Beagle from Navy, Lenny Moore of Penn State, Forrest Gregg of SMU, Bob Pellegrini from [the University of] Maryland, Sam Huff from West Virginia—who, incidentally, played guard that game. Most of those guys went on to big careers in the NFL. But we were no match for the Cleveland Browns. [Lou] Groza kicked, like, four field goals, and we lost [26–0]. But it was a real thrill coming from a smaller college and getting a chance to take part in it.

"Winning is living. Every time you win, you're reborn. When you lose, you die a little."

—GEORGE ALLEN

STAN JONES

I got started playing organized football as a freshman in high school in Lemoyne, Pennsylvania, just after World War II. After three years on the varsity, I won a football scholarship to the University of Maryland. I wasn't really familiar with the school; in fact, all I knew about it was that they had played Delaware and a couple of teams in Pennsylvania.

Jim Tatum was the coach there then, and he was a fine one. We had some very good football players on those Maryland teams: Dick Modzelewski, a tackle who went on to star for the Giants and a couple other teams; Jack Scarbath, an All-American quarterback [who] almost won the Heisman Trophy, but didn't do all that well in the pros; Chet Hanulak, who [later] played halfback for Cleveland; and Dick Nolan, a defensive back afterward for the Giants, who went on to become head coach of the 49ers and the New Orleans Saints.

In the three years I played there [1951–1953] we had, I think it was, 22 boys go on to play pro football. In my last year, we won the national championship. We were undefeated [10–0–0], but when we went to the Orange Bowl, we lost to Oklahoma.

ROCKY BLEIER

[They] rescheduled my visit [to Notre Dame] for Friday, March 13 [1964] . . . a perfect day to meet the previously unknown coach Parseghian.

Running back Robert "Rocky" Bleier, No. 20, was one of the most popular of the Steelers Super Bowl champions of the seventies, despite the fact that at 5'9" and 210 pounds, he was on the small side for a pro football player, and he wasn't especially fast. He ran for 51 yards in Super Bowl X, including the play pictured here, with left guard Jim Clack (No. 50) blocking.

One of the hardest hitters ever to play the game of professional football, Bears middle linebacker Dick Butkus (No. 51) applies the crunch to a Packers ball carrier during a game between the long-standing rivals in the early seventies. A first-round draft choice out of the University of Illinois in 1965, Butkus went to eight Pro Bowls and was named All-Pro seven times during his nine-year career in Chicago.

Ara [Parseghian] was overwhelming to me. He had that dark, Armenian face, the firm chin, wavy black hair flecked with gray, and those piercing, deep-set eyes. He *looked* like a head coach. He had such a presence in one-to-one conversation, especially on his own turf. He impressed me that day, and later, as being extremely well organized. All through the interview, he took notes in longhand on a yellow legal pad . . . notes which he filed and retain[ed] in his office. He began the conversation rather dramatically.

"We offer less than the NCAA permits," Ara said, "so if you're looking for something under the table, I'll close my books right now and end the discussion. Once you sign the grant, it's yours for four years. We don't take it back if you're injured or don't play well. We give room, board, tuition, and books. We don't give the $15-a-month laundry money, but we have our own laundry on campus, and we'll give you tickets for it."

DICK BUTKUS

So as I visited a number of other Midwest schools—Purdue and Iowa among them—Illinois kept coming up bigger and bigger, due mainly to the salesmanship of [coach Pete] Elliott. . . . I believed them when they said that Illinois, then at the bottom of the Big Ten, was going to flex its muscles for the first time in years. Another factor in the Butkus-Illinois equation was my brother, Ronnie. He had gone to Illinois and knew it to be the right place for his kid brother; but, not entirely relying on his filial powers over me, he enlisted the one-and-only Ray Nitschke, ex-Illini and all-everything linebacker for the Green Bay Packers, and after a weekend of those two beating the Illini war drum in my ear, I was so fired up that I signed a letter of intent with Illinois, which bound me to accept no other offer from a Big Ten school.

TERRY BRADSHAW

LSU [Louisiana State University] turned up the heat and began to recruit me heavily. . . . When I failed the LSU entrance exams the first time, that became my out for not attending there. They asked that I give the entrance exam another try. But the next time I took it, I doubt if I got one question right because I didn't read them: just went right down the list and made a Christmas tree. I wanted out of the LSU pressure cooker. . . . I found all kinds of reasons for not going to LSU, but the most legit was the lack of a pro-style passing attack. . . .

At Tech [Louisiana Tech University], coach Joe Aillet believed in the pro system. It all added up: I had to be a Louisiana Tech Bulldog. And guess what? I was able to pass the entrance exam without a hitch. Louisiana Tech turned out to be perfect for me: small school, personal attention, small crowds, small-time schedule. No media to speak of, no TV, and no interviews. It was just what I needed: a chance to play and mature. Except for one thing: the program was sort of in a shambles, the players weren't very good, and the attitude wasn't very healthy in the first two years.

ANDY ROBUSTELLI

Most kids who like football start just about the time they find out they can throw one. That's the way it was with me. I started in Stamford, Connecticut, where I grew up. . . . I played football in high school, and after that I went into the navy. I was 18 at the time and this was during World War II. I ended up a "water tender," a "snipe"—that's one of those guys below deck who fires the boilers. I was in for two and a half years and spent most of the time on a ship out in the Pacific.

After the service I went to a little college in Milford, Connecticut, named Arnold, which no longer exists. I got out of the service about six or seven months

Steeler Terry Bradshaw (No. 12) throws over Vikings linebacker Jeff Siemon in Super Bowl IX at Tulane Stadium in New Orleans in January 1975. It was the first of four Super Bowls in which Bradshaw quarterbacked the Steelers to the NFL championship (IX, X, XIII, and XIV). After starring for Louisiana Tech, he was a first-round draft choice of the Steelers in 1970 and led the team for a total of 14 seasons. In this championship game he guided Pittsburgh to a 16–6 victory over Minnesota.

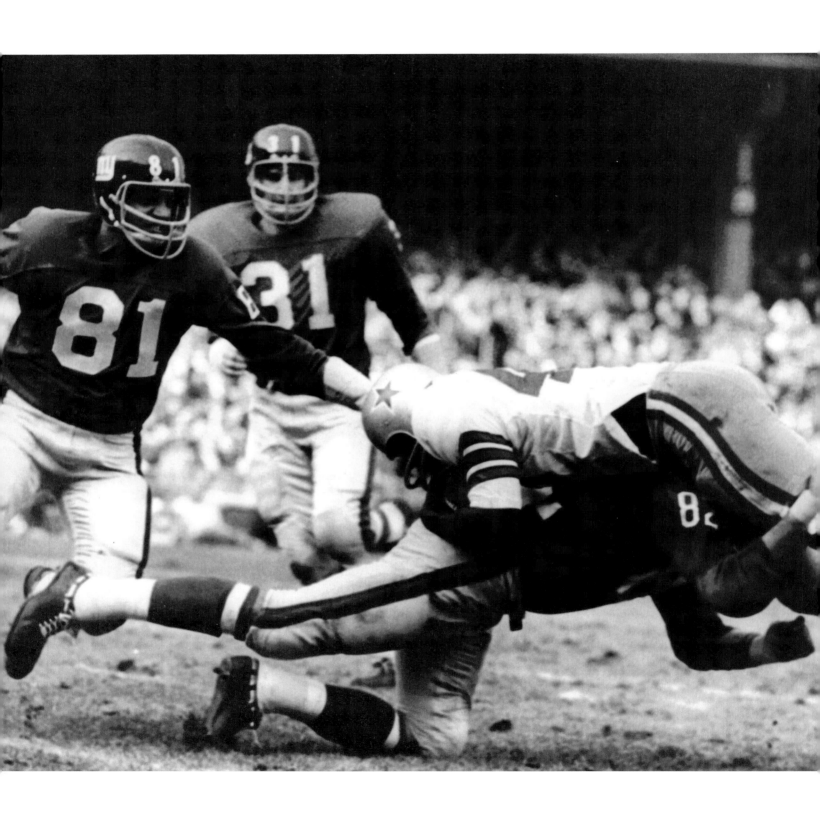

after the war ended, early 1946. Most colleges around were crowded with veterans who had already returned from the war. I think I could have gotten into Fordham, but they wanted me to go to a prep school to pick up a couple of credits. Before graduating from high school, I'd gone to LaSalle Military Academy for three months prior to going into the service. I had to wait until I was 18 before enlisting, so by doing that I missed a few high school credits, and that's what Fordham wanted me to make up.

A couple of my buddies were going up to Arnold College because they were having difficulty getting into the better-known colleges too. I went along with them. I was on the GI Bill of Rights, and so at Arnold, they said come on in. It was primarily a phys-ed school, but before there were about 200 girls and only about 40 boys. With the veterans now coming in, it ended up with more boys and less girls, about 350 students in all.

I decided to enroll, and once there, it gave me the opportunity to play any sport I wanted to. So I played football and baseball. We played against schools like the Coast Guard Academy, St. Michael's [College] in Vermont, Adelphi [University] on Long Island, and a lot of teachers' colleges. It wasn't the greatest competition in the world, but still it was tough football.

I was headed more toward baseball when I was at Arnold, and I thought—or hoped—I might get something in that sport when my college days were over. As it turned out, I did have the chance of going with the baseball Giants in New York. There was an offer. They had a Class B team in Knoxville, Tennessee, which is where I would have gone. . . .

[After graduation] I had the choice of the Giants' minor league team, a couple of high school teaching job offers, and a tryout with the Rams. I decided to go to California and try to make the team. . . . When I made the team in Los Angeles, that made the decision for me. I signed with the Rams—no signing bonus, just a plane ticket to get out there. My first-year salary was $4,250, about $350 per [regular-season] game.

CHARLIE WATERS

I was a baseball player in high school in North Augusta, South Carolina, and learned that if I didn't play football, I wasn't going to get a scholarship to college. I began as an end, but was switched to quarterback. We played for the state championship, but didn't win it. I got some publicity from it, and I was actively recruited by Georgia. My brother was already at Clemson on a baseball scholarship, and they offered me one for football. So I took it.

I played quarterback in my sophomore year. We were pretty good in the ACC [Atlantic Coast Conference], but we had a hard time outside the conference. In my junior year, I started the first four or five games, but then I broke my toe—one of those AstroTurf toe injuries—and the guy that played quarterback in my place did really well. When I came back, they moved me to wide receiver, and that worked out really well, and that's what I played throughout my senior year.

One game, we were playing Alabama, and I caught 11 passes that day. After one of them, I was tackled on the sideline and ended up at the feet of Bear Bryant. I got up and shook his hand. I said to him, "I don't know if you know this or not, but you recruited me. Sort of. But you never came to South Carolina. If you had, I would've come to Alabama."

I was invited to the Hula Bowl, where all the pro scouts go, but couldn't play because I got hurt in the last game of our regular season. I heard from Green Bay that they wanted to draft me as a wide receiver. But on draft day I got a call from Gil

Cowboys safety Charlie Waters (No. 41) applies a shoulder to Packers receiver John Thompson in this match-up in 1980. Waters, a quarterback and subsequent wide receiver at Clemson before coming to the NFL, was converted to a defensive back after being drafted by Dallas in 1970. His noble Cowboys career came to an end with his retirement after the 1981 season. Also adding impact is Dallas cornerback Steve Wilson (No. 45).

The ultra-elusive Marcus Allen (No. 32) picks up some yardage for the Raiders in this game against Green Bay. Allen, one of the illustrious line of great running backs from Southern Cal and a Heisman Trophy winner (1981), brought his extraordinary ball-carrying skills to Los Angeles in 1982 and earned Rookie of the Year honors. A Raider for 11 years, a Kansas City Chief for another five, an NFL MVP, and a Super Bowl MVP (XVIII), he proved to be one of professional football's truly great runners.

Brandt at the Cowboys, and he said, "We just drafted you as a defensive back. Do you think you can backpedal?" I said, sure, and that's how I became a safety.

> "Football is only a game.
> Spiritual things are eternal.
> Nevertheless,
> Beat Texas."
> —Sign outside the First Baptist Church of Fayetteville, Arkansas, 1980

MARCUS ALLEN

I knew Notre Dame was an excellent school, but I had no interest in going there. The more I heard about the winters in Nebraska and Michigan, the less enthusiasm I had for their schools.

I did travel to Norman, Oklahoma, though, to look at the University of Oklahoma and get better acquainted with its coach, Barry Switzer. He was a likable, laid-back kind of person with a reputation not only as an excellent coach, but as one who genuinely cared about his players. And, of course, the Sooners were among the best college football teams in the country. What intrigued me most, however, was the fact that coach Switzer had been the only one to recruit me as an offensive player. He said I would be his next triple-option quarterback. . . .

[But] in Southern California there have historically been two legendary athletic programs. The UCLA Bruins had one of the finest basketball teams in the nation, while across town, the USC Trojans could always be counted on to be among the best in college football.

From the moment USC expressed interest in me, I knew where I would go to school. I had watched them on television as a kid, memorizing the names of their great players, trying to imagine what it would be like to wear one of those cardinal-and-gold uniforms and play in front of eighty thousand people in the Los Angeles Coliseum.

JOHNNY MORRIS

I played a little bit in junior high school out in Long Beach, California, and some in high school, but I didn't really blossom until I got into college.

I played halfback on offense and defensive back for the University of California at Santa Barbara.

It was, in a way, a stroke of fate that I got into pro football. In my senior year out there, 1957, our coach got sick, and he was replaced by Ed Cody, who had played fullback for the [Chicago] Bears back around 1950 and for the Green Bay Packers before that. Well, I had a good season, and the year before that, I'd tied the [world] record for the 50-yard dash.

In those days they did not have the scouting combines like they have now, nor was the scouting nearly as organized within a club's organization. [Bears owner George] Halas had gotten many of his players by word of mouth from Bears alumni or other football friends around the country. That's what happened with me. Ed Cody called Halas and said, "Hey, I've got a little guy out here who I think can make it in the pros."

If Cody had not called him, I'm sure I never would have played professional football. Nobody scouted Santa Barbara in those days. And I was quite small—I weighed about 170 pounds and was 5'10".

Bears flanker Johnny Morris (No. 47), shaking hands with his battery mate, quarterback Rudy Bukich, came to Chicago in 1958 as a halfback from the University of California at Santa Barbara. As coholder of the world record in the 50-yard dash (5.2), Morris left his mark on the NFL as a pass receiver. When he finally called it quits after the 1967 season, Morris owned practically every Bears pass reception record.

Lyle Alzado (No. 77), shown here with Green Bay running back John Brockington, came from obscure Yankton College in South Dakota to leave a profound mark on the NFL. A defensive end best remembered for his bone-rattling tackles and devastating pass rushes, he played eight years for Denver (1971–1978), three for the Browns in Cleveland (1979–1981), and a final four with the Los Angeles Raiders (1982–1985). Alzado died of brain cancer at age 43, seven years after retiring.

LYLE ALZADO

My junior varsity coach, Mr. Hillen, had connections at New Mexico State . . . so I was all set to go there. Then they sent a letter back saying they didn't want me. It was probably a combination of things. My grades and my record in the streets. They did some checking around and found out I'd been in jail overnight a couple of times. That must have turned them off. . . .

"Bring in all the letters you got from every school," [my high school coach, Mr. Martilotta] said [afterward. We] went through them. Yankton College in Yankton, South Dakota, stood out. Little place. Peaceful. Farms and pastureland. Southeast corner of the state, 60 miles west of Sioux City, Iowa, 150 miles north of Omaha. Aggressive football recruiting campaign going on . . . especially interested in Easterners. Perfect place to hide a troublesome New York kid.

"Lyle," Martilotta said, "you're going to Yankton."

I didn't know where the hell the place was. I thought it was in Alaska. I just got on the bus. I didn't tell anybody because some of my friends would have made fun of me—the kind of guys who were jealous of anybody going to college, anybody who wouldn't end up on the corner, like them. The bus ride took 28 hours. I slept. There were only three other people on that bus.

The place was small, very desolate, a few nice, little brick houses, but no building over three stories high. The gymnasium was a converted airplane hangar. The football stadium held five hundred. The coach, Don Birmingham, met me. Nice little guy. Young, intense. He took me into a restaurant and bought me lunch—hamburgers, milk shake—a typical New York meal. I didn't want to leave the place after that.

And here's a funny thing. The place coach Birmingham took me for lunch that first day was Kip's—owned by an uncle of the girl I eventually married.

I got there on September 29, 1967. The team had already played two games. I had to attract attention quick, so I started fights. Pretty soon I was playing defensive end, at about 210 pounds. . . . My senior year I was 290. I was in the weight room all the time, lifting enormous weights, packing the pounds on.

66

Jerry Kramer, guard, place-kicker, Green Bay Packers 1958–1968.

Joe Montana, quarterback, San Francisco 49ers 1979–1985, Pro Football Hall of Fame induction 2000; Bill Walsh, head coach, San Francisco 49ers 1979–1988, Pro Football Hall of Fame induction 1993.

Gale Sayers (left), running back, Chicago Bears 1965–1971, Pro Football Hall of Fame induction 1977; Paul Hornung (center), halfback, place-kicker, Green Bay Packers 1957–1962, 1964–1966, Pro Football Hall of Fame induction 1986; Fuzzy Thurston, guard, Baltimore Colts, 1958, Green Bay Packers, 1959–1967.

Roger Staubach, quarterback, Dallas Cowboys 1969–1979, Pro Football Hall of Fame induction 1985.

70

Ray Nitschke, middle linebacker, Green Bay Packers 1958–1972, Pro Football Hall of Fame induction 1978.

Johnny Unitas, quarterback, Baltimore Colts 1956–1972, San Diego Chargers 1973, Pro Football Hall of Fame induction 1979.

Willie Wood, safety, kick returner, Green Bay Packers 1960–1971, Pro Football Hall of Fame induction 1989.

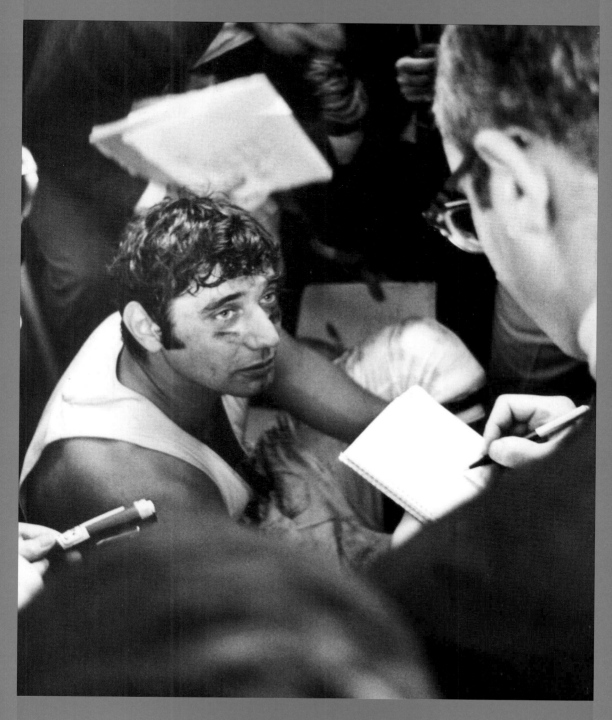

Joe Namath, quarterback, New York Jets 1965–1976, Los Angeles Rams 1977, Pro Football Hall of Fame induction 1985.

74

Mike Ditka, tight end, Chicago Bears 1961–1966, Philadelphia Eagles 1967–1968, Dallas Cowboys 1969–1972; head coach, Chicago Bears 1982–1992, New Orleans Saints 1997–1999, Pro Football Hall of Fame induction 1988.

Don Meredith, quarterback, Dallas Cowboys 1960–1968.

Don Shula, defensive back, Cleveland Browns 1951–1952, Baltimore Colts 1953–1956, Washington Redskins 1957; head coach, Baltimore Colts 1963–1969, Miami Dolphins 1970–1995; Pro Football Hall of Fame induction 1997.

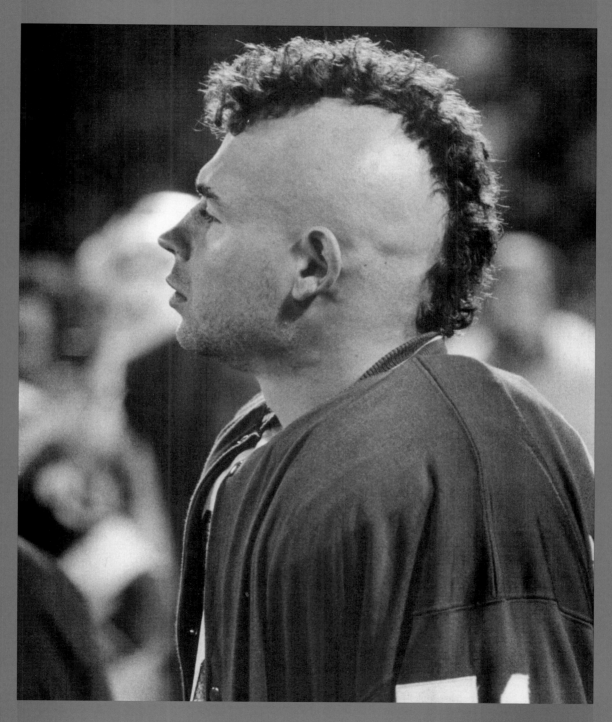

John Riggins, running back, New York Jets 1971–1975, Washington Redskins 1976–1979, 1981–1985, Pro Football Hall of Fame induction 1992.

Merlin Olsen, defensive tackle, Los Angeles Rams 1962–1976, Pro Football Hall of Fame induction 1982.

Pete Rozelle, NFL commissioner, 1960–1989, Pro Football Hall of Fame induction 1985.

Hall of Famer Jim Brown carries the ball for Cleveland in the 1965 NFL championship game against the Packers. Besides being the greatest rusher of his era, Brown was also feared as a receiver and kick returner, and he never missed a single game during his nine years in the NFL.

Alex Karras, one of the Lions' most memorable defensive linemen, looks annoyed as he awaits the next play. After a college career at Iowa, Karras played defensive tackle for Detroit from 1958–1970, missing 1963, however, because of a suspension for gambling.

Remembering the Great Ones

> "I wouldn't set out to hurt anybody deliberately, unless it was important, like a league game or something."
> —DICK BUTKUS

Over the years, the game of football has produced an amazing cast of star performers and memorable personalities, not to mention some certified characters who defy categorization. Just as baseball has its Babe Ruth, Joe DiMaggio, Willie Mays, Ted Williams, and Mark McGwire, basketball its George Mikan, Bob Cousy, Magic Johnson, Larry Bird, and Michael Jordan, football—both on the college level and in the National Football League—has its own legends, names that will forever be associated with the greatness of the sport.

From the earliest days of Jim Thorpe, Red Grange, Ernie Nevers, Bronko Nagurski, and Don Hutson, the parade of stars has been phenomenal: Sammy Baugh, Otto Graham, Frank Gifford, Jim Brown, Paul Hornung, Bobby Layne, Gale Sayers, Joe Montana, Walter Payton, Jerry Rice—the list goes on and on. They left their mark on the sport with their performances on the field, and still others made their unique impressions with their unorthodox and entertaining personalities. Among such uninhibited souls have been the likes of Johnny "Blood" McNally, Art Donovan, Alex Karras, Pete Gent, Thomas "Hollywood" Henderson, and "Neon" Deion Sanders.

Every player who has played the game of college or professional football has his own personal memories of the players he teamed with and those he went up against, the coaches who tutored them, and the deep and lasting friendships that were made. There is, in their stories, love and hate, admiration and denigration; the tales of their feats on the field and their behavior off the field, encyclopedic in volume, are about as entertaining as any football fan could ever want.

In the following pages many of those remembrances are extolled and preserved, told by the players who were there, who personally experienced or observed them. Special memories of such unforgettable players as Eugene "Big Daddy" Lipscomb, Doug Atkins, John Riggins, Jack Tatum, Merlin Olsen, "Mean" Joe Greene, and Brian Piccolo are shared. It is here the reader will find Dick Butkus on Jim Brown, Ken Stabler on Dick Butkus, Phil Simms on Lawrence Taylor, Tony Dorsett on Roger Staubach, Marcus Allen on Lyle Alzado, and Conrad Dobler on a host of personal enemies.

The views expressed come from the heart, and they offer insights into some of the most famous—and eccentric—players ever to pick up a football.

ALEX KARRAS ON EUGENE "BIG DADDY" LIPSCOMB

My own recollection of Lipscomb is vivid. He had to be the most intimidating figure in pro football history. I never could see too well without my glasses, but, on or off, the mere sight of him quickened my heartbeat, set the adrenaline flowing, and made me take off in the opposite direction. I'd take an oath on it—the man stood 7'9", weighed 8,217 pounds, breathed fire, and farted the same way.

All of which means that ballplayers were scared out of their shoes when he showed up for a game. Especially the guys who had to play against him. Opposing linemen called him "sir," and asked him about his family, his dog, and how things were going at home. Once in a while, this helped to ease Lipscomb into a docile state, but not for long. He had this peculiar fetish, this basic instinct, that separated him from all other defensive tackles in the NFL: *he came out to kill you!*

RAY NITSCHKE ON JIM BROWN

Jimmy was a fullback, but he ran more like a halfback. That was how Cleveland used him. Normally, a halfback is the one who runs the wide plays, the speed plays, and he needs more deception and more breakaway speed than a fullback usually has. Most fullbacks are the bruising type of player like Jim Taylor, a fellow who can hit the line and make it bend. The Bronko Nagurski or Clarke Hinkle type of guy. By the seventies, we began seeing more combination halfback-fullback types of runners. But in 1965 it was more unusual to see a fullback like Brown, who was better going off tackle or around the end than through the line, a fullback who played the position with great finesse. He had speed. He was adept at using his blockers. He was the smartest runner I've ever played against. Brown didn't just take the ball and start running with it and hope things worked out. He knew where his teammates were, where his help was coming from, who was going to block for him. He knew how each defensive player was going to attack him. For certain opponents, he'd just drop his shoulder and run over them; for others, he'd use his forearm to protect his legs; for

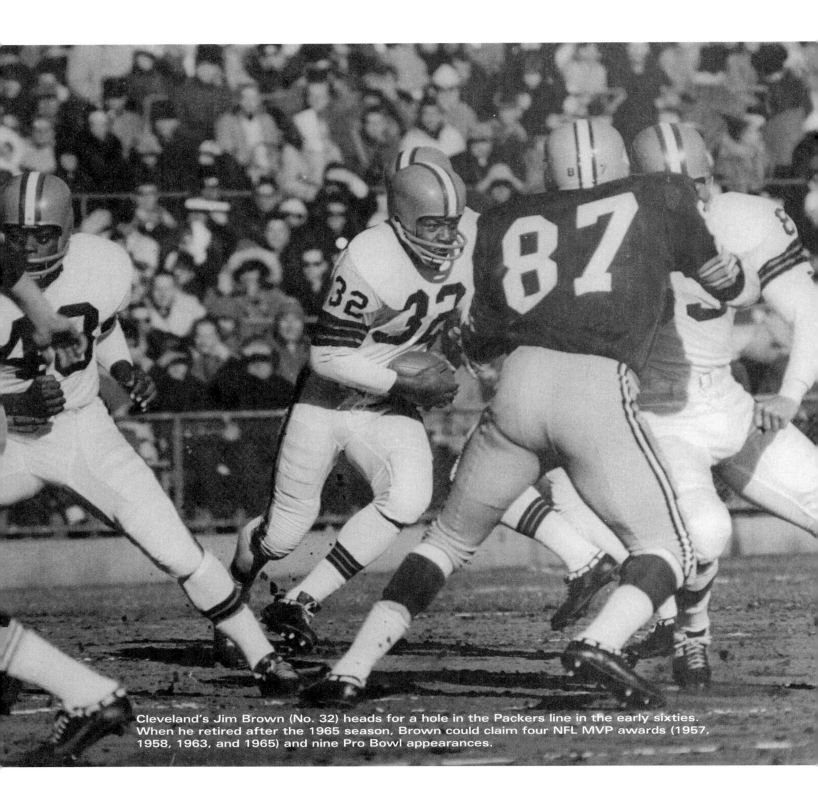

Cleveland's Jim Brown (No. 32) heads for a hole in the Packers line in the early sixties. When he retired after the 1965 season, Brown could claim four NFL MVP awards (1957, 1958, 1963, and 1965) and nine Pro Bowl appearances.

still others, he'd use finesse and quickness to outrun them. He had a sixth sense that told him how the defense would react. Then he'd react accordingly. He was an artist— a brilliant football player who could beat you not only physically, but mentally.

DICK BUTKUS ON JIM BROWN: COLLEGE ALL-STAR GAME, 1965

Of my 14 tackles, a few were applied to Jim Brown, and yes, he *was* tough to bring down, his body harder and stronger than most. He was the most agile runner I would ever face, capable of reducing the angle of almost any tackle. During the first half, the heat was almost overwhelming, but Jim just kept coming. . . .

There is one thing about that game that I will never forget. It happened late in the fourth quarter after the night had cooled down. We had put on a blitz. I shot the gap between the left guard and tackle, and there, standing between me and the quarterback, was Jim Brown, the man who, according to the sportswriters, never bothered to block. Well, he was waiting for me *that* night.

When we made contact, we seemed to freeze for an instant before I started to make a move to get by him. Suddenly he had my left arm clamped under his left arm, and when he began to roll to his left, I realized that if I didn't get my arm out of that vise Jim had it in, he'd either hyperextend my elbow or break the arm altogether.

I slipped free just in time.

Why did he do it? I don't know. Maybe he didn't like the way I hit him earlier in the game. But deep down I think it was because he was Jim Brown. He was not going to let me get by him, even though it was just an all-star game. Like all great athletes, Jim had a hidden reserve he called up in special moments.

> "Every time I tackle Jim Brown, I hear a dice
> game going on in my mouth."
>
> —DON BURROUGHS

TONY DORSETT ON ROGER STAUBACH

Now, Roger Staubach, who really *was* a guy in a white hat, was in a class by himself. He was a true Christian. People thought that because he was such a religious guy, he probably didn't have much personality. But he had a *lot* of personality, and unlike most other guys, Roger could have a good time without drinking, smoking, or cursing. And one of the things I liked about him was that he never tried to push his religion on anybody.

One of the best things about being in Dallas during my first three years was coming into contact with Roger. I told him he was my hero, and I probably have more respect for him than anyone I ever played with. I guess it's a cliché to call him an officer and a gentleman, but that's what he is. There were times when I thought if I had been white, I could have followed in Roger's footsteps in Dallas. I could have been the next Roger Staubach, and he and I could have wound up owning Texas.

PHIL SIMMS ON LAWRENCE TAYLOR

Talk about abilities! You're talking about Lawrence Taylor. Football is such an emotional game. And it's about having tremendous preparation during the week, getting ready to play. And energy, he brought energy, brought it to the team; it rubbed off on the other players. We had energy when we prepared, and we had energy when we played.

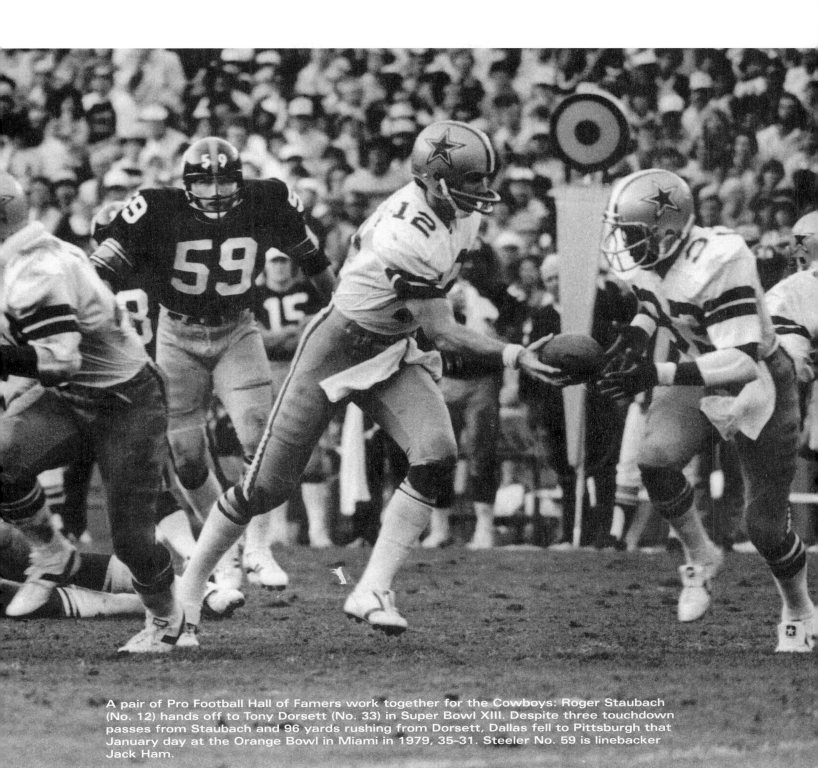

A pair of Pro Football Hall of Famers work together for the Cowboys: Roger Staubach (No. 12) hands off to Tony Dorsett (No. 33) in Super Bowl XIII. Despite three touchdown passes from Staubach and 96 yards rushing from Dorsett, Dallas fell to Pittsburgh that January day at the Orange Bowl in Miami in 1979, 35–31. Steeler No. 59 is linebacker Jack Ham.

Giants quarterback Phil Simms (No. 11) lets fly with a pass in the preseason Hall of Fame game in Canton, Ohio, in 1985 against Houston. The following season, Simms, who had quarterbacked at Morehead State in his college days, led the Giants to an NFL championship with a victory in Super Bowl XXI; he was also named the game's MVP. Blocking for him here is guard Billy Ard in a game the Giants won 21-20.

Everybody's All-Pro linebacker Lawrence Taylor (No. 56) moves in on Denver quarterback John Elway in Super Bowl XXI at the Rose Bowl in Pasadena in January 1987. Taylor, out of the University of North Carolina, joined the Giants in 1981 and earned Rookie of the Year honors. During his 13-year career in New York, he was named All-Pro nine times and went to 10 Pro Bowls. The Giants took the world championship that day at the Rose Bowl, defeating the Broncos, 39–20.

His talent was extraordinary. He made great plays. People around him would say, "Hey, you gotta try hard, otherwise you'll look absolutely horrific standing next to Lawrence." You hear all the time in basketball that Michael Jordan made his teammates look better. Larry Bird, the same. Well, that's what Lawrence did with the Giants.

And another thing about Lawrence: he was untouchable. So good a player, he was virtually untouchable. At practice, for example, hell, I had to take things from [coach Bill] Parcells basically every day. And other players did, too. We just got destroyed verbally by him, but Lawrence was so good of a player that there was nothing to get on him about. He actually could give it to the coach . . . and, man, did we love listening to him giving Bill a hard time.

TERRY BRADSHAW ON JOE NAMATH

I loved Namath for his style, because he had a way about him that was admired by everybody from the ladies to the media. I remember when I went over to introduce myself to "Broadway" Joe. He had a cop on each side of him, and the girls were screaming, and I said, "Now *there's* my idea of a quarterback."

I rarely got to play against Joe because it seemed that every time we had a game with the Jets, he was hurt. The one game he did play against us, he did poorly. When the fans booed him, he gave them the finger. Joe could handle fans. He was cool.

JOE NAMATH ON JOE NAMATH

I very rarely tackle and I almost never block. (Ever see me throw a block? I'm a regular matador; I wave my cape and step away.) I pass. And I could pass all day. I've figured out that in the past 15 years, I've thrown a minimum, an absolute minimum, of two hundred fifty thousand passes. No matter what you've read in the gossip columns, there's nothing else in the world that I've done a quarter of a million times.

Jets quarterback Joe Namath (far left) passes in an AFC game in the early seventies. The star of Super Bowl III when he led the Jets to an upset victory over the Colts, "Broadway Joe," as he came to be known, also became the first quarterback ever to pass for 4,000 yards in one season (1967).

94

His mild countenance belies the ferocity for which Doug Atkins was known on NFL fields in the sixties. A defensive end for the Browns (1953–1954), the Bears (1955–1966), and the Saints (1967–1969), the 6'8", 260-pound Atkins had a reputation for being as wild off the field as he was on the field. He is best remembered for leapfrogging blockers and panicking, if not demolishing, quarterbacks and running backs alike. Atkins was All-Pro four times and went to eight Pro Bowls.

MIKE DITKA ON DOUG ATKINS

The best story about Doug [Atkins] is the night we came in from a night out in Rensselaer, Indiana, at training camp. Doug and some guys were down in Rich Kreitling's room throwing darts. We came in after being out at the local establishment. We had had a few beers. Everybody was crowded around and got into this dart thing. The dartboard was setting up on a desk by the window. [Ed] O'Bradovich came in and said, "Hi, big guy, whaddaya doing?" Then O.B. start[ed] fooling around.

Doug said, "We're playing darts. Behave."

O.B. said, "Hey, let me show you how to throw those darts."

O.B. grabbed some darts and started throwing them. He was missing and fooling around.

Doug said, "Don't do that. We're throwing darts."

Doug grabbed the darts back. Ed grabbed one and threw it. Then he grabbed another one and threw it.

Doug said, "Cut it out."

Finally, Ed grabbed one and threw it. It missed the board, broke the window, and went out the window.

Doug grabbed Ed. Ed weighed 250 pounds. Doug picked him up over his head and threw him on the floor. The floor was made out of tile. That was it. Like a little dog, Ed got up, crawled away, and everybody disappeared. Nobody said anything. I was standing in the doorway and I went right down the hallway and went to my room. Not a word was said. It was like, "Uh-oh. The big guy has spoken."

DICK BUTKUS ON DOUG ATKINS

For whatever reasons, Atkins was usually allowed to do his thing. During weekday practices at Wrigley, for example, when the defensive unit would be running drills in preparation for Sunday's game, Atkins would hang out with the groundskeepers, trading jokes and helping them sweep up. [Bears coach George] Halas and [defensive coach George] Allen would be working the offense and defense at their respective ends of the field, and there would be Dougie in the stands with a broom in his hands. When his services were absolutely necessary to a particular play or defensive scheme, one of the coaches would request his presence and he'd disengage from the groundskeepers and shamble onto the field. I don't remember hearing anyone complain about Doug's special treatment.

"It was an amazing thing lining up next to Dobler for six years. Ten of us would be involved in a football game, and there would be Conrad having his own private little war."

—DAN DIERDORF DURING AN

ABC *MONDAY NIGHT FOOTBALL* BROADCAST

BART STARR ON PAUL HORNUNG

Paul Hornung, our halfback, was capable of heroic feats on the football field. In our 45–7 rout of Baltimore in the fourth week of the 1961 season, he reached the pinnacle. He rushed for 111 yards on only 11 carries, ran for three touchdowns, caught a touchdown pass, kicked a 38-yard field goal, and converted six extra points. The term *versatile* is generally overused, but not when describing Paul's unique skills.

Packers great Paul Hornung (No. 5) slops through the mud during the 1965 NFL title game against the Browns at Lambeau Field in Green Bay. "Golden Boy," as he was called, ran for one touchdown and rushed for a total of 105 yards that afternoon to help the Pack to a 23–12 victory. A Heisman Trophy winner from Notre Dame, Hornung was switched from a college quarterback to a Hall of Fame–bound halfback by Vince Lombardi.

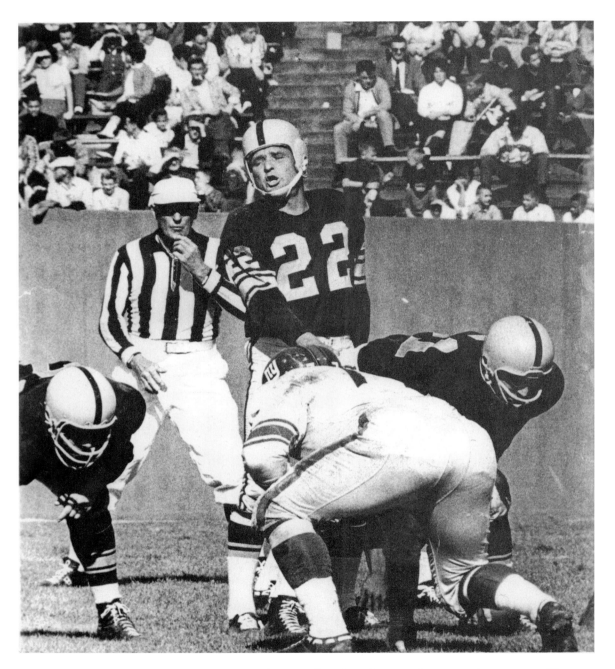

Bobby Layne (No. 22) calls out signals for the Steelers in a 1959 game. Layne, an All-American from the University of Texas, played one year for the Bears (1948) and another for the New York Bulldogs (1949) before establishing himself as one of the pro game's greatest quarterbacks with the Lions (1950–1958) and the Steelers (1958–1962, traded to the Steelers during the 1958 season). Renowned as a clutch player and famous for his two-minute drills on the field, he was equally infamous for his roistering off the field.

His achievements on the playing field were no match for his nighttime conquests, however. His "golden boy" title was appropriate yet incomplete. One year Paul traveled to the West Coast to play in the Pro Bowl. His roommate was Bill George, the Chicago Bears middle linebacker. If Bill had any thoughts of getting to know Paul, they were quickly dashed when he discovered that Paul gets warmed up around the time everyone else falls asleep. "My only roommate that week was Paul's suitcase," Bill laughed.

ALEX KARRAS ON BOBBY LAYNE

Now I think of him at practice and remember the way he'd grind his jaws, then spit, clap his hands, and bring the guys into a huddle. "Awraht, men," he'd yell in that back-country Texas twang of his. "Let's git it going, heah? Snap. Snap. Make it count." Then he'd go to work and never break a sweat. And I'd reel around under the sun and wonder what I was doing on the same field with him.

He was the baddest, best pro football player of my time. He feared nobody. Sooner or later he'd find a weakness in a player and capitalize on it. . . . It might take him two periods, or three, or into the final seconds to get his points when he absolutely had to. He would often throw short decoy passes, just to see the defensive reaction. When the victim—a cornerback, tackle, linebacker, somebody—broke down once too often, Layne knew exactly where to strike. Bam! It was as though he was riding on the pulse of unnatural movement, propelled by an invisible force.

"Bobby Layne called on Tuesday night to have a drink and we didn't get home until Saturday."

—FRANK GIFFORD

BOBBY LAYNE AND JOHN HENRY JOHNSON

According to sports columnist and author Bob St. John, [Bobby] Layne made a close friend in fullback John Henry Johnson, who would visit him in Lubbock after they both retired. Unfortunately, Bobby found out John Henry had a great fear of snakes. So one day Bobby taped a grass snake inside the huge fullback's pants. Everybody calmly watched as Johnson put on the pants, discovered the snake, and started hopping around, trying to get the pants off. When the tiny snake was shaken loose, Johnson then took off, knocking down a whole bank of lockers as he tried to get out of the dressing room.

ROCKY BLEIER ON BOBBY LAYNE

In the pros, I encountered various styles. Dick Shiner was always berating us: "Why didn't you catch the ball?" or "Who missed his block?" Bobby Layne was like that, they told me. He literally kicked guys off the field if they weren't playing well for him. Only once in his life was he at a loss for words in the huddle. At the 1959 Pro Bowl, he was so hung over from a night out, he couldn't remember the plays. Frank Gifford, a halfback, called signals for the Eastern Conference.

CONRAD DOBLER ON PETE ROZELLE

Rozelle has an aura of power. One look and you know he's the commissioner—the number one man of the number one spectator sport in America. Still, I've always had a hard time trusting someone with a year-round tan who lives in New York.

KEN STABLER ON DICK BUTKUS

We were ahead by a touchdown in the fourth quarter and driving for another score that would lock up the win. This was only a year before Butkus' bad knees forced him to retire and he could no longer move around that much, but he still hit like a tank. I had heard he was ornery. But it seemed like the more mobility he lost, the meaner he got.

We got a first down on the Bears 5-yard line. I handed off to Pete Banaszak up the middle, and he banged down to the 3. Center Jim Otto came back to the huddle looking a little woozy after his collision with Butkus. So I handed off to Pete over left guard Gene Upshaw to about the 1. Pete Banaszak had the best nose for the end zone of any back I ever played with. On the third down I gave him the ball again over the right side, and he drove in there as Butkus charged. We all thought Pete had crossed the goal line.

The referee came in and placed the ball down inches shy of the goal line. I ran over to him. "Hey, ref, what the hell are you doing? He was in. What the hell's he gotta do?"

From behind me came a voice that sounded like it was talking into a drum: *"He's got to get across the goddamn goal line!"*

I looked around and Butkus was standing right behind me, looking like Conan the Barbarian, wearing Bears jersey No. 51.

"My knees look like they lost a knife fight with a midget."

—E. J. HOLUB

Houston quarterback Kenny Stabler goes to hand off to one of the NFL's great running backs, Earl Campbell (No. 34), in an early eighties game. Campbell, a consensus All-American and Heisman Trophy winner from Texas, was the first selection in the 1978 draft. He rewarded Houston not only by leading the league in rushing and earning Rookie of the Year honors, but also by being honored as the NFL's MVP. After six full seasons with the Oilers, he finished out his career in New Orleans, retiring after the 1985 season.

One of the most fearsome sights any NFL back would encounter in the sixties and early seventies was that of the grim-faced, savagely posed middle linebacker Dick Butkus (No. 51) of the Bears. Credited with 22 interceptions and 27 fumble recoveries during his nine seasons in Chicago, he was forced into retirement after the 1973 season by a devastating knee injury.

DON MEREDITH ON PETE GENT

Pete had a tendency to take a little bit of artistic license in his interpretation. You know: if it sounds good, put it down on paper. But Pete was a good pal, and I spent quite a bit of time with him. He was very bright. He was primarily a basketball player, but he was a good football player, too—not great speed, but really good hands, and he was good coming across the middle, and if you find somebody who will go across the middle for you, you've got something pretty valuable.

I think, to a certain degree, he captured the whole business with that *North Dallas Forty* [book]. He captured a certain feeling that was there, and it was, in my opinion, a fairly accurate portrayal—with, of course, the artistic license he took.

CONRAD DOBLER ON MERLIN OLSEN

Perhaps my most talked-about one-on-one match-up was against Merlin Olsen, the Los Angeles Rams' Hall of Fame defensive tackle, in 1976. First, a little background. Merlin and I had previously tangled in the Cardinals' playoff loss to the Rams after the 1975 season. I managed, through my aggressive style of play, to temper some of the joy he felt over advancing in the postseason tournament. As a perennial all-pro, he simply wasn't used to the rugged treatment he had gotten from me that day in the Los Angeles Coliseum. But, hell, it was a playoff game—there was no tomorrow—and I was going to do everything in my power to help keep our season alive. That meant punching Olsen in the stomach. That meant leg-whipping him in the vicinity of his crotch. That meant taking advantage of the fact that he was 10 years older, and thoroughly manhandling him. He was so furious after the game, he told the press, "I won't send flowers if someone breaks Dobler's neck."

Pete Gent played flanker, wide receiver, and tight end for Dallas from 1964 through 1968 and entertained everyone (with the exception perhaps of the Cowboys front office) with his irreverent sense of humor. His most lasting legacy, however, was the novel he wrote, *North Dallas Forty*, a ribald romp behind the scenes of a fictitious pro football team most people recognized as the Dallas Cowboys.

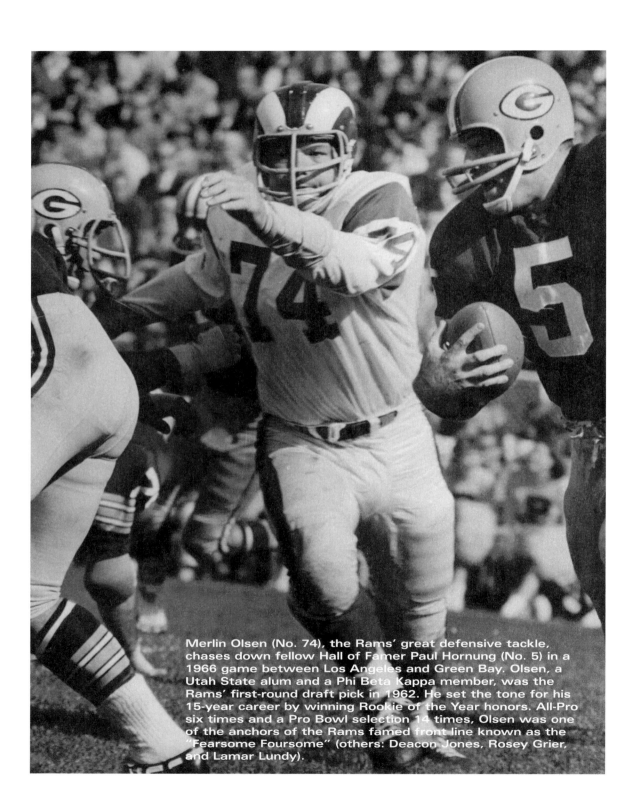

Merlin Olsen (No. 74), the Rams' great defensive tackle, chases down fellow Hall of Famer Paul Hornung (No. 5) in a 1966 game between Los Angeles and Green Bay. Olsen, a Utah State alum and a Phi Beta Kappa member, was the Rams' first-round draft pick in 1962. He set the tone for his 15-year career by winning Rookie of the Year honors. All-Pro six times and a Pro Bowl selection 14 times, Olsen was one of the anchors of the Rams famed front line known as the "Fearsome Foursome" (others: Deacon Jones, Rosey Grier, and Lamar Lundy).

JOE NAMATH ON ABNER HAYNES

There's one guy who's not with us anymore I can't forget—Abner Haynes, who joined us after the 1967 season started. In one game against Kansas City, I gave the ball to Abner, and he got hit right at the line and spun around, and he looked up and lateraled the ball to me. I had no choice: I had to catch the ball. And then I saw "Big" Ernie Ladd, all 295 pounds of him, coming at me, and I ducked and Ernie went right by me. Then I started running, running for my life, and when there was just one man between me and going all the way, I got knocked out of bounds.

[Jets coach] Weeb [Ewbank] pulled Abner right out of the game, and Clive Rush [an assistant coach] phoned down to the bench and talked to Abner and said, "Abner, we just don't have that play in our playbook. We just don't do that." I wasn't upset. Hell, I got up laughing. I guess it was kind of nervous laughter; I was glad I was still alive.

ART DONOVAN ON JOHN RIGGINS

I guess John Riggins of the Redskins was the closest guy I've seen to those old-timers. Riggins is the kind of guy who, as we used to say in the marines, got hit in the head one too many times with a hand grenade. But I've yet to see Riggins or anyone else in modern football mix it up like we used to do. Thank God.

CHARLIE WATERS ON WALTER PAYTON

One game against the Bears, they ran an end run against us, and Walter was coming my way. I played off the lineman [blocker] perfectly. And I had Payton in my sights. All my job was was to turn the play in, but I got off my guy and saw I could make the tackle myself—had him dead to rights. I lunged for him, came up with nothing, hit the ground, and looked up.

John Riggins (No. 44) carries for a Redskins touchdown in Super Bowl XVII despite the clinging effort of Miami cornerback Don McNeal (No. 28). Riggins, the game's MVP, rushed for 166 yards that day as Washington defeated the Dolphins, 27–17. Riggins carried the ball for the Jets for five years before joining the Redskins in 1976; he remained in Washington through the 1985 season (except for 1980, which he sat out), virtually rewriting the team's rushing record book. No. 86 on the Redskins is tight end Clint Didier.

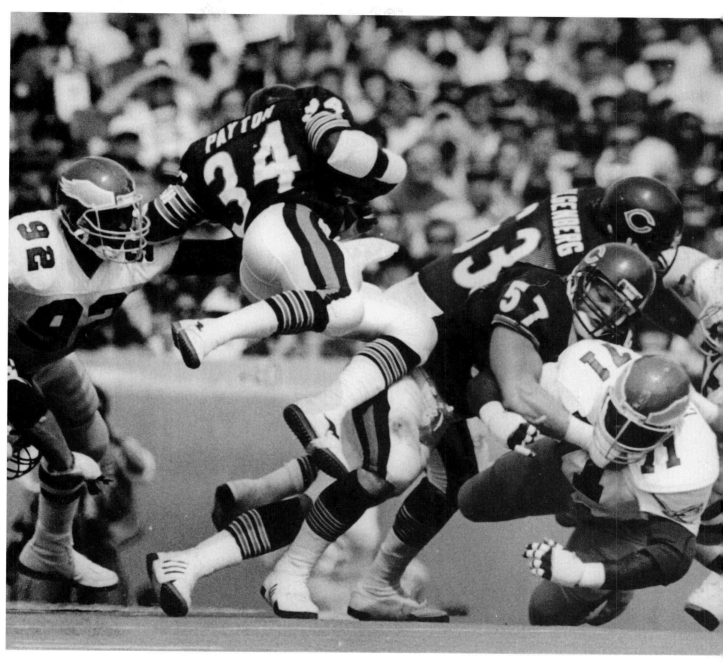

The soaring Walter Payton (No. 34) dives for a few of the career 16,726 yards he gained for the Chicago Bears during his career with the team (an NFL record until Emmitt Smith broke it in 2002) in a game against the Philadelphia Eagles. Payton, a first-round draft choice out of Jackson State in 1975, held seven NFL and 28 Bears records when he retired after the 1987 season. Blocking for him here are center Jay Hilgenberg (No. 63) and guard Tom Thayer (No. 57).

He had reversed field and was heading downfield. I got up and chased the son of a bitch all the way down the other side of the field and came in from behind him. I was coming in from his blind side and I knew I was going to kill him—no way could he see me. And I'll be damned if he didn't dodge me again—and I know he didn't see me. And I missed him again.

I mean, I could go five or six games without a missed tackle, and here I got two missed tackles on one play because of the great Walter Payton.

GEORGE BLANDA ON PAUL W. "BEAR" BRYANT

My first impression of [Bear Bryant] when he came down in January of my freshman year [at Kentucky, 1946] was, "This must be what God looks like." He was a very handsome man, tall and smooth. He was the most energetic man I'd ever seen. He'd walk in the room and you wanted to stand up and applaud. He gives this speech to the student body and I thought he was going to get elected president. . . .

[He] was a wonderful coach and a wonderful man . . . a mean son of a bitch, but a wonderful coach and man. The Bear taught me discipline, respect, and dedication. He'd run your fanny right into the ground. Those practice sessions of his . . . well, when they were over, you wanted to collapse.

But the Bear wasn't that merciful. He wouldn't even let you die. He'd make you run back to the locker room. He'd tell you to turn in your suit if you didn't sprint.

I picked up a lot from him. He was just as mean as my old man. But they both taught me how to compete.

RAY NITSCHKE ON GALE SAYERS

Sayers was the finest instinctive runner I've every played against. He ran like a rabbit, with a rabbit's quickness and ability to change direction while the hounds went thundering past. Once, watching the films when we were getting ready to play Chicago, I saw him make a play that I couldn't believe.

He went off tackle. He left the ground on his left foot. But he couldn't put his right foot down because there was a pileup ahead, and if he'd put that foot down someone would have reached out from the pile and grabbed it. So instead of landing on his right foot, he landed on his left foot—the one he'd taken off on—and it was only after he was clear of the pileup that he put that right foot down. Then he regained his balance and scooted away from there.

"He looks no different than any other running back when he's coming at you, but when he gets there, he's gone."

—GEORGE DONNELLY, ON GALE SAYERS

DICK BUTKUS ON GALE SAYERS

Gale would take a kickoff or a deep punt and start downfield, eluding the first tackler and the second, and with the crowd noise swelling, he'd cut to the sideline or across the middle and turn on the afterburners. Then we would all be on our feet, ready to kick ass by the time he was tackled or driven out of bounds or had scored. He was instant adrenaline to all of us. Every time Gale touched the ball, you knew in the back of your mind that you might be witnessing something that might never happen again. Gale's running was pure creativity, and I have never seen his like since.

From day one back at training camp, [Bears coach] Abe Gibron had me on the kickoff return team. At first he put me at the point, but sometimes when I peeled back I tended to knock my own men down as the wedge—four of us, shoulder to shoulder to protect the ball carrier—turned back on itself to pursue the ball carrier as he sought a sideline lane. Later he put me farther back in the wedge. This allowed me to see the field better and make strategic blocks to free up Gale. As I watched the ball spiraling over my head, I would tell my team, "Wait . . . wait . . . " When Gale had gathered the ball in his arms and was five yards behind us, I'd yell, "Go, go, go!"

It was everyone's job to hit at least one man as the wave of defenders converged on Gale. The trick was to time our blocks just as Gale arrived. When it worked—as it so often did—it was beautiful to experience. I don't know how many times I found myself on my ass after a block, watching Gale burn one player after another, leaving them strung behind like so many disabled vehicles.

> "If they don't want them to get hit,
> why don't they just put a dress on 'em?"
>
> —JACK LAMBERT, ON PROTECTING QUARTERBACKS

CONRAD DOBLER ON WILLIE LANIER

Probably the toughest overall defender I ever played against was Kansas City Chiefs linebacker Willie Lanier. I rarely laid a lick on him. He was just so fast and had such great lateral movement. At the time I played against him, Willie was nearing the end of his career, while I was a fairly young man. But that didn't matter. In addition to maintaining his great speed, he also had great knowledge of the game and would always take the fastest route to the point of attack.

One of the game's most elusive running backs, if not *the* most elusive, Chicago's Gale Sayers (No. 40), aptly nicknamed the "Kansas Comet" while starring for the University of Kansas, electrified pro football fans with his dazzling runs from scrimmage and on kickoff returns. As a rookie in 1965 he set a record with 22 touchdowns (since broken) and tied another when he scored six touchdowns in one game against the 49ers. Injuries to both knees forced him to retire after just seven seasons.

Because I was still in the learning stages, I had a hard time trying to find the right spot to make the cut-off block. But one time I did, bringing Willie to the ground. As we both were falling, he swung an elbow into my chest that I can still feel to this day.

"Willie, now why would a nice guy like you go and do a thing like that?" I asked.

He got up laughing. "You just always seem to bring the worst out in me."

JOHN ROBINSON ON MARCUS ALLEN

I've seen running backs who were a little faster and maybe even a little stronger than Marcus Allen, but none who had his combination of intelligence and competitiveness. Those are the things that have set him apart from the rest. Add to them the God-given physical characteristics that a great back needs—balance and vision, ability to get into the holes quickly, explosion at the end of a run—and you've got the whole package.

I'd be lying if I said I expected something like the year he had as a senior, but I wasn't that surprised.

And I did know early on that he was going to be something special. I knew that the first week of two-a-day practices in his freshman year when we still had him working with the defensive backs.

I was coming out of my office one afternoon and met him in the lobby of Heritage Hall, and we stood there near the display of Heisman Trophies. As we talked, he kept glancing over at them, then finally grinned and said, "I can't win one of those playing defensive back, can I?" It was the next day that I moved him to tailback.

MARCUS ALLEN ON LYLE ALZADO

Lyle fascinated me. His background, which he openly talked [about] in a self-deprecating manner, sounded like something out of *West Side Story*. He had grown up on the mean streets of New York and had the knife-fight scars to prove it. His mom was Jewish and his father of Spanish and Italian heritage, and he survived his boyhood days because he was big and mean enough to be the neighborhood bully. By age 16, he was working as a bouncer at a bar he described as "one of those real-life bucket-of-blood joints."

His only goal in early life was to grow up to be a professional boxer. As long as you like beating the hell out of people, he'd say, you might as well get paid something for it.

TERRY BRADSHAW ON "MEAN" JOE GREENE

When I look back on my first year at Pittsburgh, with all the many things that I had to learn and endure, the one person that comes to mind first and foremost is Joe Greene. I'll never forget the first time I laid eyes on Joe coming down the hill to practice: socks down around his ankles, huge thighs, big Afro, jersey hanging out, looking like he had been up all night. What a sight! He was called "Mean" Joe Greene because he earned the name. He took cheap shots at quarterbacks, driving them out of bounds and into the bench if he could. He was ferocious. He couldn't be blocked because he was so overpowering. Joe Greene was something that the NFL had never seen before—he redefined the position of defensive tackle.

"Mean" Joe Greene (No. 75) watches the action at Three Rivers Stadium in Pittsburgh. When he was on the field, however, a tackle in the fabled "Steel Curtain" defense, he lived up to his nickname, as all running backs and quarterbacks who faced him will attest. An All-American at North Texas State, Greene was the Steelers' first-round draft choice in 1969. Through the seventies he was the mainstay in a defensive line that won four NFL championships. His Hall of Fame career ended when he retired after the 1981 season.

"Look, I'm really a nice guy. At least I try to be. Most of the time. When I'm not being hassled. I don't like it when people call me *mean*. I've always been big and strong . . . but that doesn't mean that I go around beating on people."

—"Mean" Joe Greene

CONRAD DOBLER ON "MEAN" JOE GREENE

Pittsburgh defensive tackle "Mean" Joe Greene was one of the players on whom it was difficult for me to use any form of intimidation. Going into a game against a guy hostile enough to be called "Mean" Joe, I can't say that I didn't feel a little bit intimidated myself.

During one of our confrontations, he jumped and raised his arms way over his head to try to knock down a pass. Unable to resist such a wide-open target, I hauled off and punched him right in the solar plexus. And when he came down, he yelled, "Dobler, you goddamn motherf***er! I'll kill you for that."

I went back to the huddle and started thinking, hey, this is "Mean" Joe Greene I'm messing with. This is a guy whose mental makeup isn't a whole lot different from mine.

But I wasn't completely convinced his threat was as serious as it sounded. I decided, if I got the chance, I'd try the technique one more time. Four plays later, we threw another pass and, sure enough, Greene was off his feet and stretching to get a paw on it. Once again, I was staring at that wide-open target. Once again, I hauled off with a punch. As I turned to walk away, he grabbed one of my shoulders and spun me around. I could tell, by his viselike grip, he was serious—very serious.

"What the hell's wrong with you, Conrad?" Greene yelled.

I looked at him and shrugged. "I don't know what got into me, Joe. I guess I just lost my head."

He didn't say anything. He didn't do anything. He just stared at me with death in his eyes for a few seconds, then walked away.

DOUG BUFFONE ON BRIAN PICCOLO

Brian Piccolo was [with the Chicago Bears] when I arrived [in 1966], and he became a good friend. We were in Rensselaer, Indiana [the Bears' training camp site], one day, and I got sick, and so did Brian. So Brian and I were both quarantined to the dorm. I had the flu. Brian had a slight cough and just generally was not feeling good. I got better, but he still didn't look too good even after we went up to Chicago for the regular season. One day at Wrigley Field—my locker was right next to his there— he was coughing, worse, it seemed, than when we were quarantined together. So I said, "Pic, you've got to get rid of that damn cough. Why don't you go see a doctor or something?"

He looks at me and says, "I think I got cancer."

Now Pic was always a clown, loved to kid around. So I just shook it off. . . . But then, down in Atlanta, we're playing the Falcons, and it was very hot. Pic took himself out of the game, and Pic would never come out of a game on his own. He just couldn't breathe. They took him back to Chicago and found out he did in fact have cancer.

Running back Brian Piccolo (No. 41), who starred at Wake Forest, joined the Bears in 1966. In 1969, he uncharacteristically took himself out of a game against the Falcons; a little more than seven months later he died of lung cancer. Blocking for him here is tackle Randy Jackson.

GALE SAYERS AND BRIAN PICCOLO

In May 1970 Gale Sayers flew to New York to accept the George Halas Award for the Most Courageous Athlete of the Year because of his comeback from a serious knee injury to lead the NFL in rushing. But when George Halas handed him the trophy, Gale Sayers told the large group that a mistake had been made. The award should have been given to his friend and former Bears teammate, Brian Piccolo. With deep emotion, he told them:

> Think of Brian and his courage and fortitude shown in the months since last November, in and out of hospitals, hoping to play football again, but not too sure at any time what the score was or might be. Brian Piccolo has never given up.
>
> He has the heart of a giant and that rare form of courage that allows him to kid himself and his opponent—cancer. He has the mental attitude that makes me proud to have a friend who spells out the word *courage* 24 hours a day, every day of his life.
>
> You flatter me by giving me this award, but I tell you here and now that I accept it for Brian Piccolo. Brian Piccolo is the man of courage who should receive the award. It is mine tonight. It is Brian Piccolo's tomorrow.

I love Brian Piccolo and I'd like all of you to love

him. When you hit your knees to pray tonight, please ask

God to love him, too.

Editor's note: Brian Piccolo died of cancer on June 16, 1970, at age 26.

"You felt honored to tackle him."

—MATT MILLEN, ON WALTER PAYTON

MIKE DITKA ON TOM LANDRY

I thought Landry was going to be kind of a sterile guy. I had a preconceived idea he was going to be a very sterile person. Maybe that's not the right word. I just thought he would be a plain guy with a lot of authority and not much emotion.

I was completely wrong. I think Tom has as much emotion and compassion as anybody. I saw it in meetings we had, but I saw it more when I became a coach. You really saw what made him work and what made him tick. You saw how bad he felt when he cut people.

People say he's cold. He's the furthest thing from cold. But what is he going to do? Sidle up to everybody buddy-buddy and go out and have a beer with them? You can't do that. The "plastic" image was something that came out to the public, but it certainly wasn't the truth. That bothered him. In staff meetings we saw the personality, the friendship, the jokes and laughter. We played golf with him. Other people don't see that part of him. They just see the guy who doesn't smile a lot.

Watching intently from the Dallas sideline in 1972 are two of the game's most notable figures, tight end Mike Ditka (No. 89) and coach Tom Landry. Ditka would later become a head coach himself, first for the Bears and then the Saints. Landry, who coached the Cowboys from their inception in 1960 through 1988 (a record of 270–178–6, two Super Bowl victories, and five NFC titles) was inducted into the Pro Football Hall of Fame in 1990; Ditka, as a player, was enshrined in 1988.

The joy of victory shown on the faces of Randy White (No. 54) and Harvey Martin (No. 79) at Super Bowl XII. The two defensive linemen contributed significantly that day at the Louisiana Superdome in New Orleans as the Cowboys defeated the Broncos 27–10. White, the co-MVP of Super Bowl XII, played defensive tackle for Dallas from 1975 through 1988 and nine times was named All-Pro and selected to go to the Pro Bowl.

THOMAS "HOLLYWOOD" HENDERSON ON RANDY WHITE

Randy White [was] a great football player. Aside from Conrad Dobler, who was a complete wild man, he was by far the toughest, most aggressive, reckless football player I've ever seen in my life. The guy is tough. He has no regard for whatever is coming at him; he will just attack it. Plus, because of his size, he's usually bigger than whatever he has to face. An offensive line trying to block him is like a swarm of Volkswagens trying to stop a diesel.

Linemen don't have the big opportunities to really hit people hard; they usually come and hit them with a shoulder pad or wrestle a guy down. A linebacker or defensive back gets a chance to work up a 10-yard head of steam and really cream somebody. Randy White was different; he could mangle you from a standing start. He could dish out punishment in a very confined area—the line of scrimmage. That's what he'd do all day: every series of plays he'd beat up the center and two guards.

TERRY BRADSHAW ON JACK LAMBERT

Jack Lambert was not like any rookie the Steelers ever had. At training camp the veterans tried to haze Jack, demanding he sing the Kent State fight song. It's a tradition in the NFL to make rookies sing their college fight songs. Lambert told them, "Kiss my ass, I'm not singing anything." Jack Lambert never sang. He set his tone right off the bat. Nobody intimidated Jack Lambert.

J. T. Thomas, a starting cornerback, once said of Lambert, "He's so mean he doesn't even like himself."

Steelers middle linebacker Jack Lambert slips in front of Rams wide receiver Ron Smith to intercept a Vince Ferragamo pass in Super Bowl XIV. Lambert, as mean as his teammate "Mean" Joe Greene—and some say he was a more vicious tackler— came to the Steelers from Kent State in 1974 and hung around for 11 years. He was All-Pro eight times and went to nine Pro Bowls, and he played on four Super Bowl championship teams.

126

RAY NITSCHKE ON JOHNNY UNITAS AND RAYMOND BERRY

When Raymond Berry was catching passes for the Colts, the timing between him and [Johnny] Unitas was hard to believe, even when you saw it. Berry would have his back to the quarterback when the ball was thrown, and he'd turn around and reach up and the ball was there. Unitas anticipated Berry's movements with as much intuition as a wife who's checking up on a husband. He knew that so many yards down the field, in such and such a location, Berry would be ready to catch the ball. Then he'd get it there at that precise moment. I don't say it happened that way every time—there's no such thing as perfection on the football field or anywhere else. But it happened often enough because they'd worked together on this timing until the execution was so close to being perfect that we could have two guys covering Berry and still he'd catch that ball.

"There were times when I got back to the huddle
after being hit so hard I was hearing the entire
Mormon Tabernacle Choir and a marching band
banging their drums in my head."

—TERRY BRADSHAW

ART DONOVAN ON HIS BALTIMORE COLTS TEAMMATES

We were playing an exhibition game in Milwaukee once, and a bunch of us, naturally, were drinking in a local bar. Around midnight, most of us left, but [Don] Shula

The one and only Johnny Unitas doing what he did so well. After college at Louisville, Unitas was cut by the Steelers in 1955 and joined the Colts as a free agent the following year. From there he forged a Hall of Fame career in Baltimore that lasted through the 1972 season. Respected as one of the game's greatest field leaders, Unitas quarterbacked the Colts to NFL crowns in 1958 and 1959; he was All-Pro six times and went to 10 Pro Bowls. He spent his final year in the NFL with the San Diego Chargers.

Hall of Fame wide receiver Raymond Berry gathers in a pass for the Colts from fellow Hall of Famer Johnny Unitas. Berry joined Baltimore in 1955, and when he hung up his cleats after the 1967 season, he had caught more passes than any NFL player in history, 631 (since broken). A product of Southern Methodist, Berry also was near the very top of the record lists with 9,275 yards gained on those receptions and 68 touchdown catches; he went to six Pro Bowls during his 13-year NFL career.

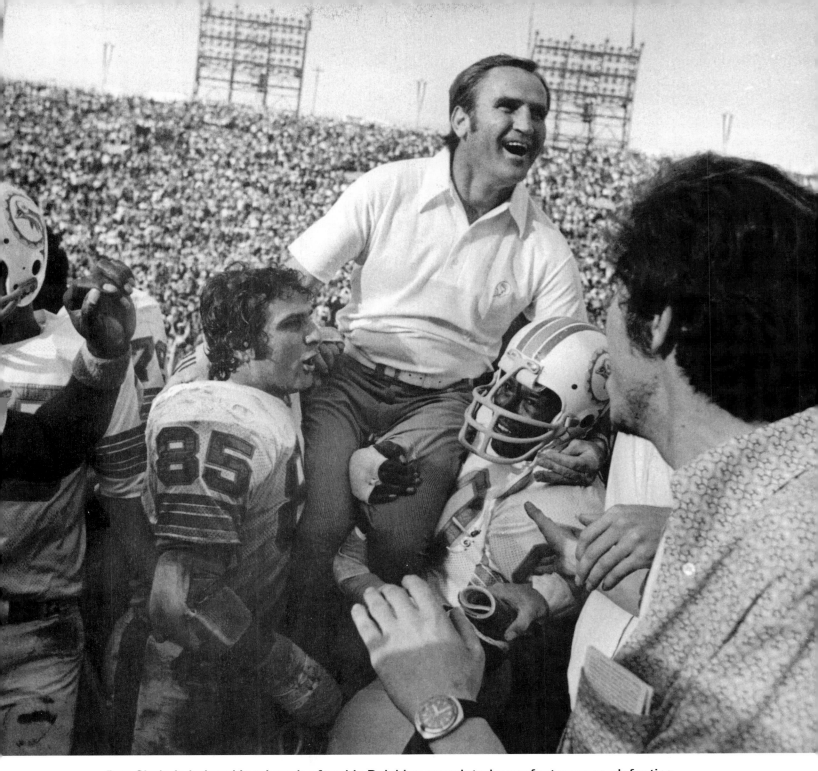

Don Shula is hoisted in triumph after his Dolphins completed a perfect season, defeating the Redskins 14–7 in Super Bowl VII. That January afternoon at the Coliseum in Los Angeles in 1973, Miami became the first (and only) perfect-record team in NFL history, achieving 17 victories without a defeat or tie. Providing a boost is Dolphins linebacker Nick Buonconti (No. 85). Shula retired from coaching after the 1995 season as the winningest coach in NFL history, with a record of 328–156–6.

stayed there with Carl Taseff, another defensive back. We were back up at the hotel for a little while when suddenly the cops showed up. Uh-oh. One officer walked up to me and said, "We know one of you Colts stole a taxicab. Who was it?"

What happened was Shula and Taseff honked the horn of a cab outside the bar, but the driver didn't show up. So Shula put Taseff, who was stewed to the gills, in the back of the cab, put the cabbie's hat on, and drove back to the hotel. And you know, they never would have gotten caught, except Taseff was slow getting out of the cab. He wanted to pay Shula the fare.

DICK BUTKUS ON GEORGE HALAS

[Bears coach and owner George] Halas was a mass of contradictions. He was the most profane man I ever knew, a man who could outcurse a platoon of drill instructors or make even Lenny Bruce sound angelic. Yet Halas was so pure when it came to sex that he could have lectured Cotton Mather. But there may have been a practical side to Halas' puritanism. He truly believed that sexual activity drained an athlete of his ability. As Papa Bear put it, "I don't want any of you guys leaving your games on some damn whore's bed!"

KEN STABLER ON JACK TATUM

Jack was real nice off the field: quiet, intense, hardly ever smiled. But nobody f***ed with Jack. I don't care if you were 6'8" and weighed 300 pounds. Jack wore a kind of permanent scowl on his face and kept a hangman's look in his eyes, and that's how he played. There was nothing dirty about his game—he stayed within the rules. He occasionally used "the Hook" that [George] Atkinson taught him, but usually he just hit with his helmet and shoulders, a 5'11", 205-pound missile. He'd run into guys with his eyes open and never blink.

The "Father of Professional Football," George Halas was there at the meeting in Canton, Ohio, when the National Football League was formulated. He then served as owner, player, and/or coach of the Chicago Bears during the game's first season in 1920 (the Bears were the Decatur Staleys that year) until his death in 1983 at age 88. During his long NFL coaching career he is credited with 324 victories, a record that would stand for three decades.

Tatum hit Broncos tight end Riley Odoms, a 6'4", 240-pounder, with a shot in Mile High Stadium that sounded like a cannon went off in that thin air. It was a stalemate, as somehow Odoms held the ball. But he was the only player I ever saw take a Tatum blow like that and not be carried off the field. Odoms just staggered off.

Intimidation was Jack's game, and he was the champion.

A LITTLE EXTRA LEVERAGE

Bob St. John, sports columnist and author, provides this insight into one of the NFL's more vicious players.

Los Angeles Rams linebacker Don Paul had the reputation of being one of the NFL's toughest, meanest players. The Lions' giant tight end, Leon Hart, 6'5" and 250, once called him the dirtiest player in the league. Paul laughed at that. He thought it was a compliment. Once Paul suffered a broken jaw one game and played in the next.

"I play the Lions' kind of football," said Paul.

"I don't hit with my fists, but when I hit a ball carrier and there's that split second before the whistle blows, I hit him again, hard.

"In the pros you know how to get that extra leverage to be able to hit hard."

THOMAS "HOLLYWOOD" HENDERSON ON MIKE DITKA

Mike Ditka is a maniac. He could coach choir girls and make them bloodthirsty champions. He is the Tasmanian devil of NFL coaches. He coaches like he played: fire in his eyes, an intensity that goes beyond concentration to pure obnoxious egotism, the kind of guy who just doesn't care who he hurts as long as he gets what he's after. And he only wants his kind of player on his specialty teams. He loves that good devastating hit, and he hates a coward.

Ditka runs his program on fear and humiliation. If you don't play well, if you don't get cut, if you don't block, if you don't tackle, if you show an ounce or a moment of cringe, he will show you up. Don't want to be pusillanimous around coach Ditka.

133

> "Bo Jackson looks like he's all muscle—that is, his ears look like they have muscles. His nose looks like it has muscles. When you see him barefoot, even his toes look as if they've got muscles."
>
> —*New York Times* sports columnist Ira Berkow

CLIFF HARRIS ON CHARLEY TAYLOR

Charley Taylor was the most fearsome wide receiver that I played against while I was with the Cowboys. We played the Redskins twice each year, and I'll tell you, he was one tough individual. He was the kind of receiver who would make the big play. And when he hit you, he would rattle your helmet—sometimes he'd knock it clear off. He broke

The Redskins' great split end Charley Taylor makes a diving catch for a touchdown in this 1973 game against the 49ers. Taylor, a first-round draft pick in 1964 out of Arizona State, earned Rookie of the Year honors as a running back; he was switched to split end in 1966. When Taylor retired after the 1977 season he had caught more passes than anyone in NFL history up to that time, 649. He went to nine Pro Bowls during his illustrious Redskins career.

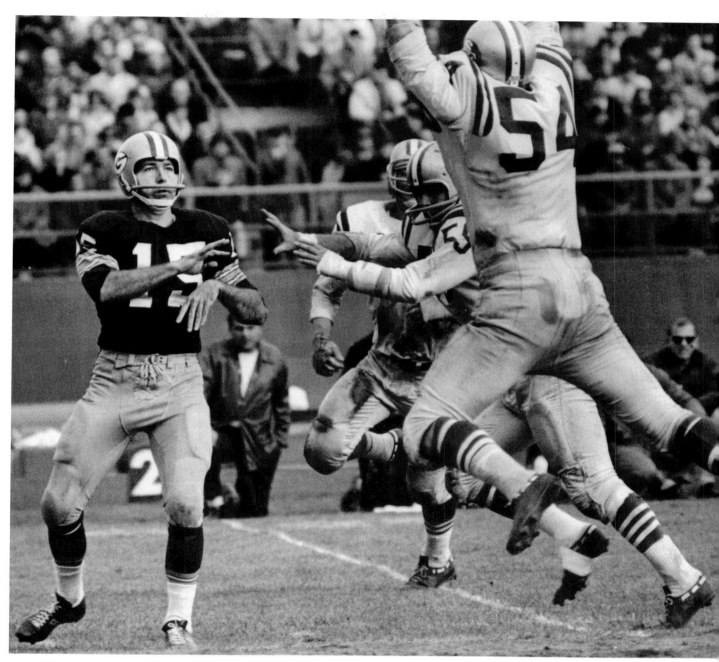

Bart Starr watches the flight of one of the many passes he threw for the Packers during the fifties, sixties, and early seventies. Hailing from the University of Alabama, Starr wasn't selected until the 17th round in 1956, but he went on to lead Green Bay to two Super Bowl victories, five NFL championships, and six division titles during his 16-year Packers career. He was selected as the MVP in both Super Bowl I and II.

[Cardinals safety] Jerry Stovall's jaw once. He almost knocked me out in one game. And he would block. You could never hurt him. Normally, as a safety, you hit a receiver and you punish him. Charley Taylor you couldn't. He'd punish you. You paid the price.

RAY NITSCHKE ON JIM TAYLOR

Early in [a game against the New York Giants], he [Packers fullback Taylor] set the pattern. When he got the handoff, he headed straight for [the Giants' Sam] Huff, who had a reputation as a tough linebacker. Sam drove him out of bounds, and as they skidded across the ice, he was using his knees and elbows on Jimmy as fast as he could.

When Taylor got up, he was groggy. I saw him staggering. He leaned over, coughing blood. But he went back to the huddle and grabbed [Packers quarterback Bart] Starr's arm.

"Give me the ball," he said.

When the ball was snapped, Bart gave it to [him]. He headed straight for Huff. He hit him like a bull moose, knocked him down, trampled him into the icy ground, and kept going. Even those New York fans cheered.

All day, he defied the Giants. He'd get smashed to the frozen turf with half the defensive team piling on top of him, and when he got up he'd turn and snarl, "Is that as hard as you can hit?"

BART STARR ON JIM TAYLOR

Jim Taylor may have been the toughest football player I've seen. He was not particularly big [5'7", 212 pounds], fast, or elusive, but he had a vicious, mean streak. He became angry every time he was tackled, which meant he was always mad at two or three defenders—one was never enough to stop him.

One of the game's greatest power runners, Green Bay fullback Jim Taylor (No. 31) steps out with ferocity in a game against the Colts. Taylor, who prepared for the NFL at LSU, was a second-round draft pick of the Packers in 1958. He gained more than 1,000 yards in five consecutive seasons (1960–1964) and was instrumental in the great success of the Lombardi dynasty in Green Bay. The Colt he has just run over is safety Jerry Logan.

Jimmy was used to overcoming adversity. When he was 10, his father died, so he began delivering newspapers at 4:00 A.M. to help support his family. While he was still in high school, he worked in the Louisiana oil fields, swinging a sledgehammer. This routine continued through his college days at LSU. He also became such a devoted weightlifter that George Allen commented, "He has the muscular structure of a 230-pound man."

At LSU Jimmy refined his blocking skills by leading the way for sophomore sensation Billy Cannon. The Packers drafted Jimmy in the second round of the 1958 draft. They had a steal.

Jimmy's background and strength led to some incidents that became legendary. Even [Packers coach Vince] Lombardi was shocked during a game when Jimmy passed up an obviously clear path to the end zone, changed direction, and blasted into a defensive back. He still scored, but Lombardi asked him, "Why did you run into him? You had a clear path to the end zone."

"You've got to sting 'em, Coach," answered Jimmy. "I figure if I give the guy a little blast, he might not be so eager to try and stop me next time."

FRAN TARKENTON ON HUGH MCELHENNY

I'll never forget the first time I saw Hugh McElhenny. . . . They called him "the king." "The king of the halfbacks." The rookies had been in camp for about a week, and the veterans were due in a few days. McElhenny drove in a day early. He showed up in the afternoon unannounced, standing in the shade under one of the pine trees, watching our workout. What a sight. He came in driving a big black Cadillac towing a trailer painted black. He was dressed in black jeans with some kind of matching T-shirt and tennis shoes that matched his outfit. He had this weathered complexion

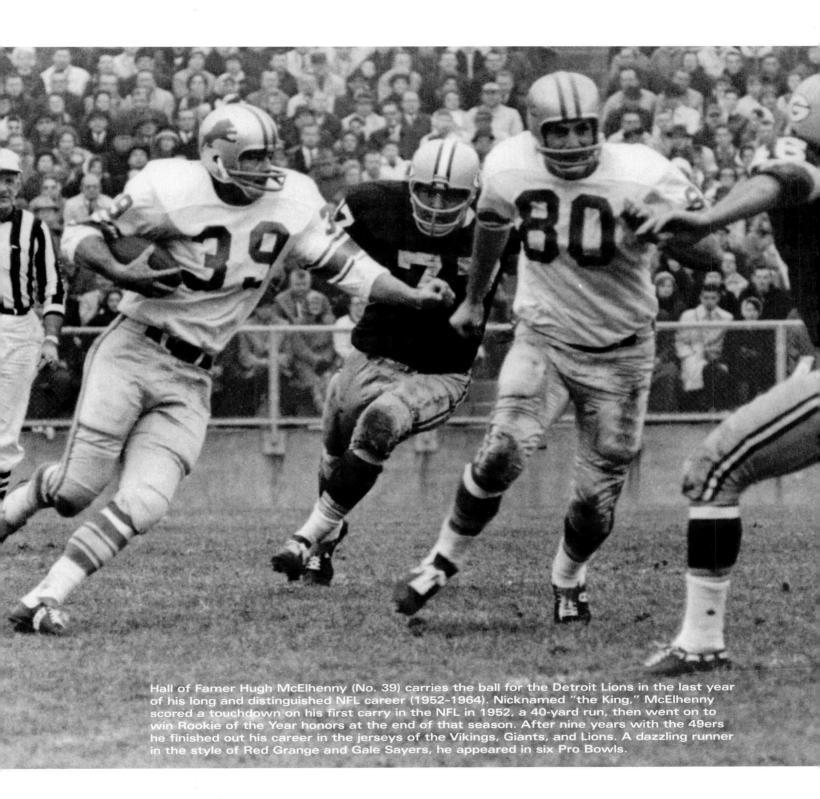

Hall of Famer Hugh McElhenny (No. 39) carries the ball for the Detroit Lions in the last year of his long and distinguished NFL career (1952–1964). Nicknamed "the King," McElhenny scored a touchdown on his first carry in the NFL in 1952, a 40-yard run, then went on to win Rookie of the Year honors at the end of that season. After nine years with the 49ers he finished out his career in the jerseys of the Vikings, Giants, and Lions. A dazzling runner in the style of Red Grange and Gale Sayers, he appeared in six Pro Bowls.

with little pockmarks and a few small scars in his face that gave it extra character. His hair was jet black, and he just stood there looking like the incarnation of the pro football star: glamour, strength, aura, whatever you wanted. All my life I had read about Hugh McElhenny.

[Coach Norm] Van Brocklin saw him and went over to where he was standing. They shook hands and gabbed for a little while, and then the Dutchman [Van Brocklin] brought him over to us and introduced him. "I want you to meet the king of the halfbacks," he said. "This is Hugh McElhenny. He's going to be one of your teammates." McElhenny waved to us like we were all going to be in the Hall of Fame inside a couple of months.

MIKE DITKA: TOUGH GUYS

The toughest guys I played against? Ray Nitschke of the Packers—he was as tough as there was. Willie Wood, up in Green Bay, was a really rugged defensive back. I had great respect for Willie. And, of course, I had to play against Herb Adderley. Another was a kid out of the 49ers—Jimmy Johnson, a great defensive back. Through my career, most of the trouble seemed to come from the Packers, guys like Willie Davis.

Another of the toughest guys I played against was Bill Pellington, at Baltimore—he'd knock people down with his fist. Gino Marchetti—I respected him so much. . . . I mean if you can block Marchetti and you can block Willie Davis, you can block anybody. Another one was Alex Karras over in Detroit. . . . There was a linebacker out of San Francisco who came later . . . Dave Wilcox. . . . I had a couple of good run-ins with Sam Huff of the Giants, but I had great respect for Sam because he played the game the way I did, and we both felt you can't worry about who gets mad at you.

141

Safety Willie Wood (No. 24) picks one off for Green Bay in the 1961 NFL title game against the Giants. His Hall of Fame–bound career began when he joined the Packers as a free agent in 1960. During the sixties Wood starred defensively and as a punt returner in two Super Bowls and six NFL title games, was named All-Pro six times, went to eight Pro Bowls, and had 48 career interceptions. The intended receiver of this pass from Y. A. Tittle is tight end Joe Walton (No. 80). Green Bay won that day, 37–0.

"When you tackle Earl Campbell, it lowers your IQ."

—PETE WYSOCKI

CONRAD DOBLER ON JETHRO PUGH

I will admit there was one Cowboy I truly respected: defensive tackle Jethro Pugh. I had some of the better games of my life against Jethro. Beat him every time we met. Maybe it was because I psyched him out with my reputation. Maybe it was because he was tall and lanky and that always allowed me to get good leverage on him. But it wasn't because he was a bad player. In fact, he was a great one. There were players I couldn't handle who didn't have half his ability. It's just that, occasionally, you get somebody's number, and I had Jethro's and he knew it. He was one guy on whom every technique I used—clean or dirty—worked to perfection. I'd get on a roll, and there was nothing he could do to beat me. There were games when he never once got near the quarterback. But I think the biggest ego-shattering moment for Jethro came when I managed to pull his jersey right over his helmet without being penalized.

THOMAS "HOLLYWOOD" HENDERSON ON CLINT LONGLEY

Our first [college] playoff game was in Abilene, Texas, against Abilene Christian University, and they were a hell of a team. Abilene Christian had a history of playing in these games; people had heard of Abilene Christian, nobody knew anything about Langston [University].

Their quarterback was a guy named Clint Longley, "the Mad Bomber." He liked to look downfield and throw the ball as far as he could see, and he had receivers who could run under it. The next year he was playing for the Dallas Cowboys. At running

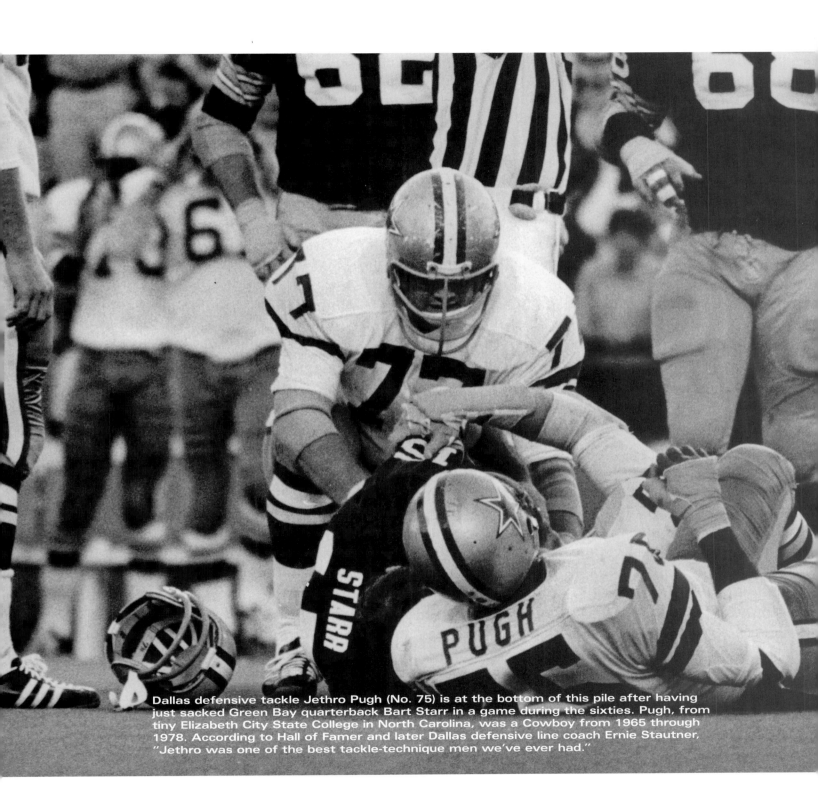

Dallas defensive tackle Jethro Pugh (No. 75) is at the bottom of this pile after having just sacked Green Bay quarterback Bart Starr in a game during the sixties. Pugh, from tiny Elizabeth City State College in North Carolina, was a Cowboy from 1965 through 1978. According to Hall of Famer and later Dallas defensive line coach Ernie Stautner, "Jethro was one of the best tackle-technique men we've ever had."

Upside down is linebacker Ted Hendricks (No. 83) as he dives over (and brings down) Packers quarterback Lynn Dickey in a 1976 game. Hendricks, a three-time All-American from the University of Miami (Florida), played for three teams during his 15-year NFL career: the Colts (1969–1973), Packers (1974), and Raiders (in Oakland 1975–1981 and Los Angeles 1982–1983). Hendricks played in four Super Bowls and seven AFC title games; he went to the Pro Bowl eight times.

back was this guy who had scored something like 38 touchdowns, name of Wilbert Montgomery. He went on to play about nine years in the NFL. Between them they put on a show.

Longley was showing off his bomb arm and Montgomery ran for four touchdowns, and we hadn't seen a football team that could play like that. They were like a real football team, with an idea about what came next and why. We were there to kick the hell out of somebody, but they really took it to us.

KEN STABLER ON TED HENDRICKS

In August 1975 [Oakland owner Al Davis] grabbed veteran linebacker Ted Hendricks from Green Bay, where he had not meshed in the Packers' defensive system. His nickname was "Kick 'em in the Head Ted" because he had no qualms about applying his feet to opponents when the urge seized him. Hendricks had no qualms about anything.

The day he reported at Santa Rosa, he didn't turn out with the rest of us for practice, and we wondered where he was. Then we saw him coming over the hill that rose just beyond the field. He was riding a horse, in uniform. Except on his head was a spike-topped World War I German helmet that he'd painted silver and black, and on the sides were Raider symbol, patch-eyed pirate decals. Everyone cheered. Hendricks rode right up to John Madden and said, "OK, Coach, I'm ready to play some football."

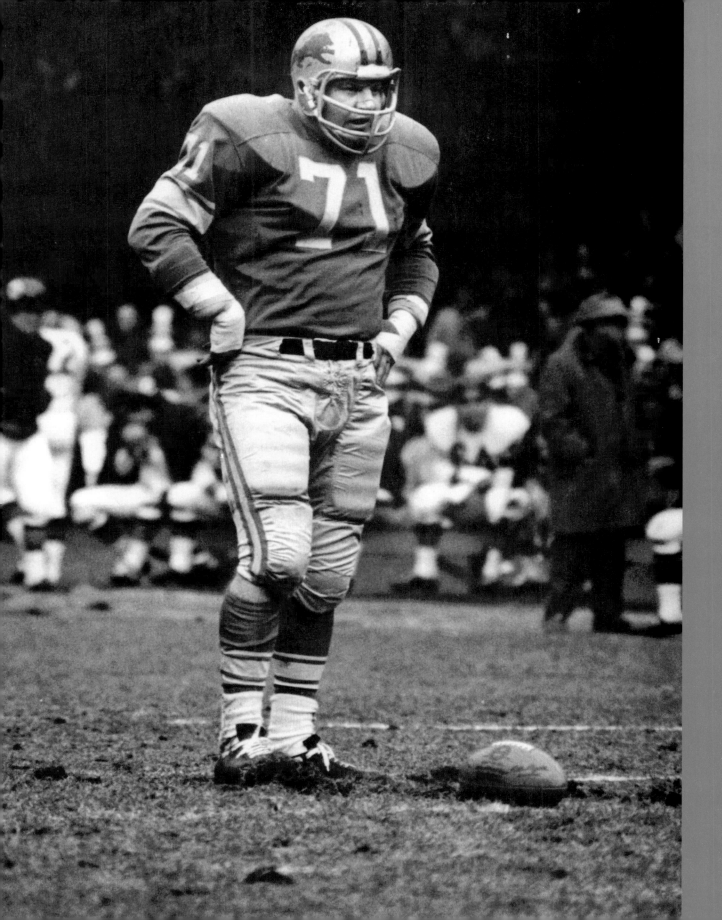

148

Alex Karras, defensive tackle, Detroit Lions 1958–1962, 1964–1970.

Vince Lombardi, head coach, Green Bay Packers 1959–1967, Washington Redskins 1969, Pro Football Hall of Fame induction 1971; Ray Nitschke, middle linebacker, Green Bay Packers 1958–1972, Pro Football Hall of Fame induction 1978.

150

Terry Bradshaw, quarterback, Pittsburgh Steelers 1970–1983, Pro Football Hall of Fame induction 1989.

Sonny Jurgensen, quarterback, Philadelphia Eagles 1957–1963, Washington Redskins 1964–1974, Pro Football Hall of Fame induction 1983.

152

Gale Sayers, halfback, Chicago Bears 1965–1971, Pro Football Hall of Fame induction 1977; George Halas, end, Chicago Bears 1920–1929, head coach, Chicago Bears 1920–1929, 1933–1942, 1946–1955, 1958–1967, Pro Football Hall of Fame induction 1963.

Jim McMahon, quarterback, Chicago Bears 1982–1988, San Diego Chargers 1989, Philadelphia Eagles 1990–1992, Minnesota Vikings 1993, Arizona Cardinals 1994, Green Bay Packers 1995–1996.

154

Norm Van Brocklin (left), quarterback, Los Angeles Rams 1949–1957, Philadelphia Eagles 1958–1960, head coach, Minnesota Vikings 1961–1966, Atlanta Falcons 1968–1974, Pro Football Hall of Fame induction 1971; Fran Tarkenton, quarterback, Minnesota Vikings 1961–1966, 1972–1978, New York Giants 1967–1971, Pro Football Hall of Fame induction 1986.

Dick Butkus, middle linebacker, Chicago Bears, 1965–1973, Pro Football Hall of Fame induction 1979.

156

Tom Landry, defensive back, punter, New York Yankees (AAFC) 1949, New York Giants 1950–1955, head coach Dallas Cowboys 1960–1988, Pro Football Hall of Fame induction 1990.

Y. A. Tittle, quarterback, Baltimore Colts 1948–1949 (AAFC), 1950 (NFL), San Francisco 49ers 1951–1960, New York Giants 1961–1964, Pro Football Hall of Fame induction 1971; Allie Sherman, quarterback, Phil-Pitt 1943, Philadelphia Eagles 1944–1947, head coach, New York Giants 1961–1968.

158

John Madden, head coach, Oakland Raiders, 1969–1978.

William "Refrigerator" Perry, defensive tackle, Chicago Bears 1985–1993, Philadelphia Eagles 1993–1994.

John Robinson, head coach, Los Angeles Rams 1983–1991.

John Riggins (left), running back, New York Jets 1971–1975, Washington Redskins 1976–1979, 1981–1985, Pro Football Hall of Fame induction 1992.

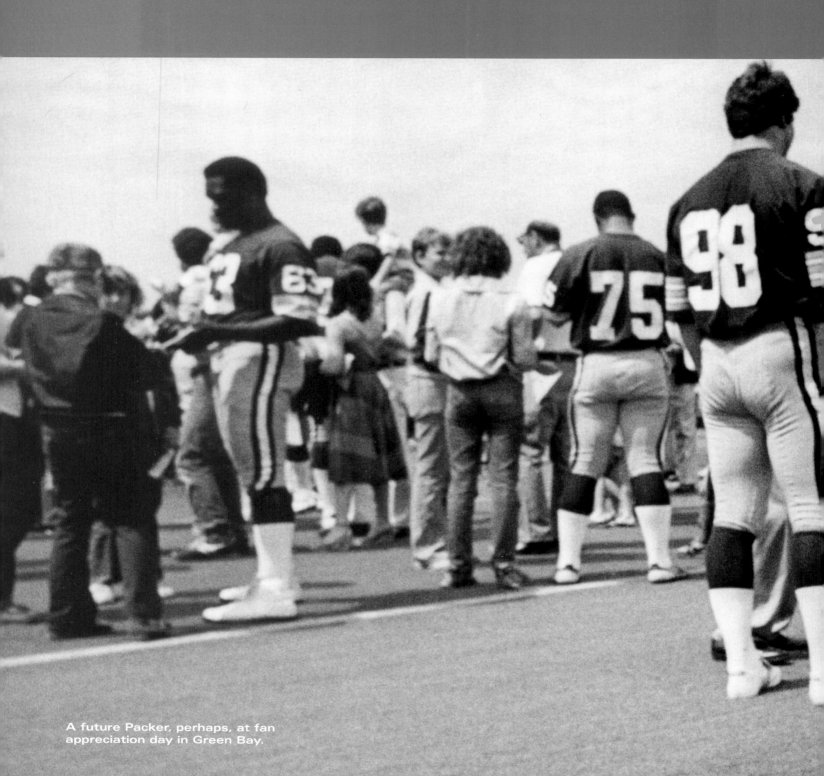

A future Packer, perhaps, at fan
appreciation day in Green Bay.

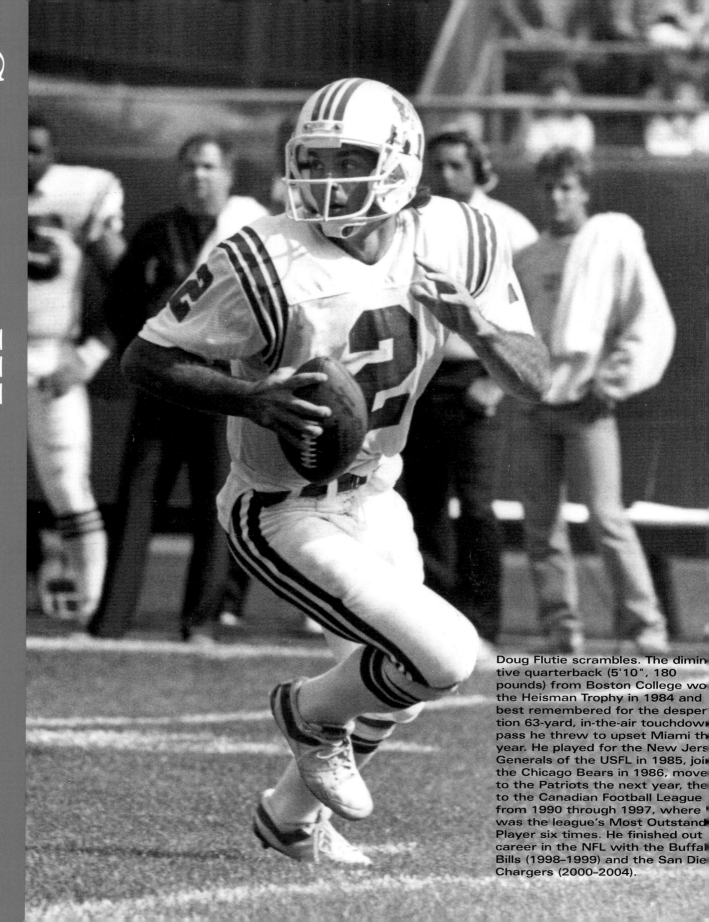

Doug Flutie scrambles. The diminu-tive quarterback (5'10", 180 pounds) from Boston College wo the Heisman Trophy in 1984 and best remembered for the desper tion 63-yard, in-the-air touchdow pass he threw to upset Miami th year. He played for the New Jers Generals of the USFL in 1985, joi the Chicago Bears in 1986, move to the Patriots the next year, the to the Canadian Football League from 1990 through 1997, where was the league's Most Outstand Player six times. He finished out career in the NFL with the Buffal Bills (1998–1999) and the San Die Chargers (2000–2004).

Behind the Scenes

"Two kinds of football players ain't worth a damn: one that never does what he's told, and the other that does nothing except what he's told."

—BUM PHILLIPS

Legendary Green Bay Packers coach Vince Lombardi summed it up in the late sixties when he said, "Football must be a game for madmen, and I must be one of them." No one knew his players better than Lombardi: Jim Taylor was the personification of toughness; Paul Hornung was the money player; Max McGee was outrageous; Bart Starr was the leader; Willie Davis was the 110 percent guy. Lombardi knew they were all distinct in their own right, they were all individuals, and he respected that in them. At the same time, as Packers defensive tackle Henry Jordan once noted, "He treats us all equally . . . like dogs."

Madmen, dogs, whatever: professional football players march to the beat of their own drummer. They are fierce, fearless, often outspoken, sometimes outrageous, sometimes withdrawn: violence and passion are the chief components in the way of life that comes with the occupation they have chosen. Left to their own devices, football would be chaos, but they are brought together as a team by coaches and blended into a smoothly running (at least most of the time), well-coordinated force that systematically tries to move a football from one end of the field to the other or tries to prevent an opponent from doing the same.

As a result, there is a boundless outpouring of stories of life within their world. But most of these tales seldom make their way out of the locker rooms or the reunions of retirees. Still, the best stories are always the ones that tell what in fact went on behind the scenes, what so-and-so really said or actually did, the glimpses of the human sides of the men we watch play the violent game of football, the wacky things they sometimes do on and off the field.

Such stories, such insights, such revelations of what went on behind the scenes are the meat of this section. Their authenticity is proven by the fact that they are told by the players themselves: Doug Flutie describes *the Pass,* so famous now in football as to warrant capitalization and italics; Art Donovan talks about the best fight he ever witnessed; Terry Bradshaw tells how he remembers the Immaculate Reception; Dick Butkus discourses on some really serious partying; Ray Nitschke recalls what it was like playing for the Packers in the golden age of Lombardi; Joe Namath reveals what he was thinking when he brashly predicted the outcome of Super Bowl III; and Thomas "Hollywood" Henderson provides his unique perspective on a bevy of things.

There are many, many more stories here, as the great and the not-quite-so-great share the moments, events, and people who motivated them, awed them, embarrassed them, and entertained them.

NFL legendary coaches George Halas (left) and Vince Lombardi talk before a game between Halas' Bears and Lombardi's Packers at Lambeau Field in the sixties. Halas, the team's owner, coached the Bears for 40 years; Lombardi, the Giants' offensive coordinator for five years before coming to Green Bay in 1959, guided the Packers for nine years and the Redskins for one before succumbing to cancer.

DOUG FLUTIE ON *THE PASS*: BOSTON COLLEGE VERSUS MIAMI, 1984

They started celebrating on the sideline, thinking they had won. We took it on the 20 with 28 seconds left, and I hit Troy Stradford on a seam route for a 19-yard gain. A holding penalty against Miami stopped the clock. I came right back and hit Scott Gieselman, who ran out of bounds at the Miami 48. I didn't even use the darn time-outs. I saved them, thinking I might need them, and wound up not using them. I threw a pass to Peter Caspariello at about the Miami 25-yard line, but it was incomplete. There were only six seconds left on the clock.

The last play of the game we called was "55 flood tip." Everybody lined up out to the right. . . .

The ball was snapped, but the play was blown dead for a penalty. But then the officials waved it off. I didn't bother rehuddling. I stayed at the line of scrimmage and yelled out the snap count. I told Peter Caspariello to go down the back side. I decided I was going to drop back, try to buy some time, roll to the right, let the guys get there, and throw a jump ball. . . .

When I rolled out to the right, I didn't have time to look to the back side. I just let it heave to Gerard [Phelan]. . . .

It's so funny to watch the tape of Gerard just chugging down the field with his head down. He didn't even bother turning around and looking until he got down to the end zone . . . although [two defenders] tipped it. Gerard said he tried to catch it in his stomach, but the ball slipped down, and he trapped it against his thigh and fell into the end zone. When he landed, he saw there was writing on the ground underneath him and knew he'd scored. Then he showed the referee he had the ball.

Officially it was ruled a 48-yard pass, but I actually threw it 65 yards. The amazing thing for me was I didn't even know who caught the ball. I saw the ball fall over the heads of the two defensive backs and thought it fell incomplete.

CHARLIE WATERS WITH AN INSIGHT INTO TOM LANDRY

He was every bit as stoic as I expected him to be. Strong, confident, he never reached around for words, never was unsure of himself; there was no questioning his authority. He made us players who put out for him.

I remember after one game where [Eagles wide receiver] Harold Jackson beat me for three touchdown passes. Awful game, I hate talking about it. Well, people talk about learning those life lessons, but I had to go to work the next day, and I lost the game. So I had to hitch my little ass up and get in there to face the music 'cause I'd got burned, burned bad.

Landry started off the meeting with, "Hey, Charlie had a rough day yesterday. Everybody here knows what he's going through." He looked around the room, then said, "But if I had 47 other players that played as hard as he did, we wouldn't ever lose a game." And I tell you, with that, he had me for life. That was it. I mean, I would run through brick walls for him.

KEN STABLER: A SHITHOUSE RAT

[Alabama coach Paul W. "Bear"] Bryant wasn't really happy about the way I did some of those good things. On the option pitchouts and pitchbacks, I'd roll behind moving blockers, and the defense would watch my eyes. When I turned my head toward the

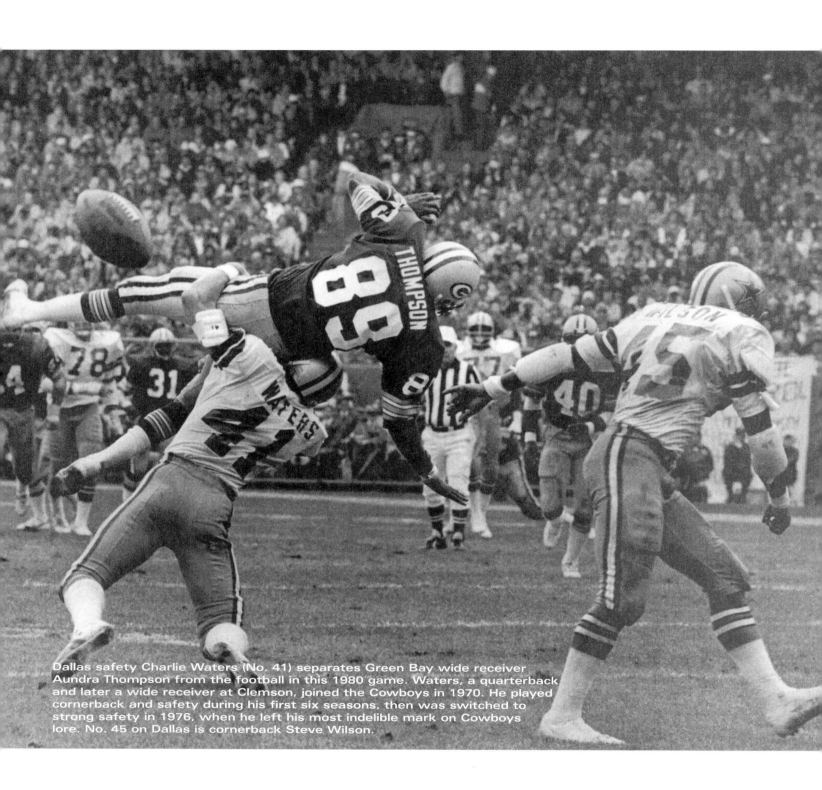

Dallas safety Charlie Waters (No. 41) separates Green Bay wide receiver
Aundra Thompson from the football in this 1980 game. Waters, a quarterback
and later a wide receiver at Clemson, joined the Cowboys in 1970. He played
cornerback and safety during his first six seasons, then was switched to
strong safety in 1976, when he left his most indelible mark on Cowboys
lore. No. 45 on Dallas is cornerback Steve Wilson.

Tom Landry was well known for his stone face and his Hall of Fame coaching career with the Dallas Cowboys. A defensive back and punter during his playing days in the AAFC in the late forties and with the New York Giants in the early fifties, he served as an assistant coach and defensive coordinator for the Giants from 1954 through 1959 before taking over the head coaching duties at the brand-new Cowboys franchise. He stayed for 29 years and established himself as one of the pro game's greatest coaches.

Kenny "the Snake" Stabler (biting his tongue, something he rarely did off the field) gets ready to hand off the ball in Super Bowl XI. Behind Stabler's quarterbacking the Raiders won the 1976 NFL championship that day, defeating the Vikings 32–14; Stabler completed 12 of 19 passes for 180 yards and one touchdown. No. 63 for Oakland is guard Gene Upshaw; No. 70 is tackle Henry Lawrence.

runner I was pitching to, defenders could read me. I decided to take away that key. I knew where my runner was going to be on every play and didn't have to look at him. I'd just pitch to that spot while looking straight ahead. We picked up a lot of yardage on runs off those blind pitches, as defenders were slower getting to the ball carriers.

But every time I made a blind pitch, no matter what we gained, coach Bryant would be waiting for me on the sideline. "Stabler," he'd say, "you're luckier than a shithouse rat!"

ART DONOVAN: NOW THIS WAS A FIGHT

The best training camp fight between teammates I've ever seen took place in front of sixty-two thousand people. . . . It was between [Eugene] "Big Daddy" Lipscomb and an offensive guard by the name of Ken Jackson, and it was one of the most brutal fights I've ever seen. Big Daddy got the shit kicked out of him.

To be frank, Big Daddy was pretty much a bully as a football player. Baltimore brought him over from the Rams in 1956, and for all the legends that grew up around Big Daddy, he never really played for Los Angeles except on special teams, when they would send him in to try to block a kick. He was 6'6", about 290 pounds, and I don't think he liked to hit. . . .

The other protagonist in this drama, Ken Jackson, the "Tall Texan," was a man of long memory. . . .

Jackson had this fight with Big Daddy up in training camp. Actually it wasn't really a fight. Big Daddy took a sucker shot at Jackson and decked him. By the time Jackson scrambled back up into the fray, there were people already breaking it up, so Jackson never really got any licks in. But he turned to Big Daddy and said, "I'm gonna get you, you dirty bastard. You're dead meat." No one doubted that he meant it.

174

Every year, the Colts would play an intrasquad exhibition game for the benefit of various Baltimore charities—the Boys Club and whatnot—and sixty-two thousand fans would fill Memorial Stadium. So the 1957 game was perhaps three weeks after the fight, and nothing had happened between Big Daddy and Jackson. Then, right in the middle of the game, Jackson did it. He butted Big Daddy—broke his face mask, shattered his nose, and knocked a couple of teeth out. They dragged Big Daddy off the field, unconscious. And when he woke up on the bench he began mumbling, "I'm gonna kill that Texas bastard. I'm gonna go back in there and kill him."

Jackson heard about it, went over to Big Daddy on the sideline, and told him, "I hope you come back for more. 'Cause I ain't through with you yet. I'm gonna murder you." And he had this gleam in his eyes that really shook Big Daddy. Hell, it shook me, too.

We went up to Big Daddy and told him, "Gene, stay away from that guy. He will kill you." And from that day on Big Daddy avoided the Tall Texan like the plague.

"If you play one regular-season game in the National Football League, you will never, ever, be normal physically."

—JOHN MADDEN

DICK BUTKUS ON THE ROSE BOWL

To many of the Los Angeles folks, football was only a small part of the Rose Bowl. We were on display every afternoon and evening: going to Disneyland, posing with Mickey Mouse, and on to Knott's Berry Farms. This was all fine and good, except that we were supposed to be getting ready for the biggest football game of the year.

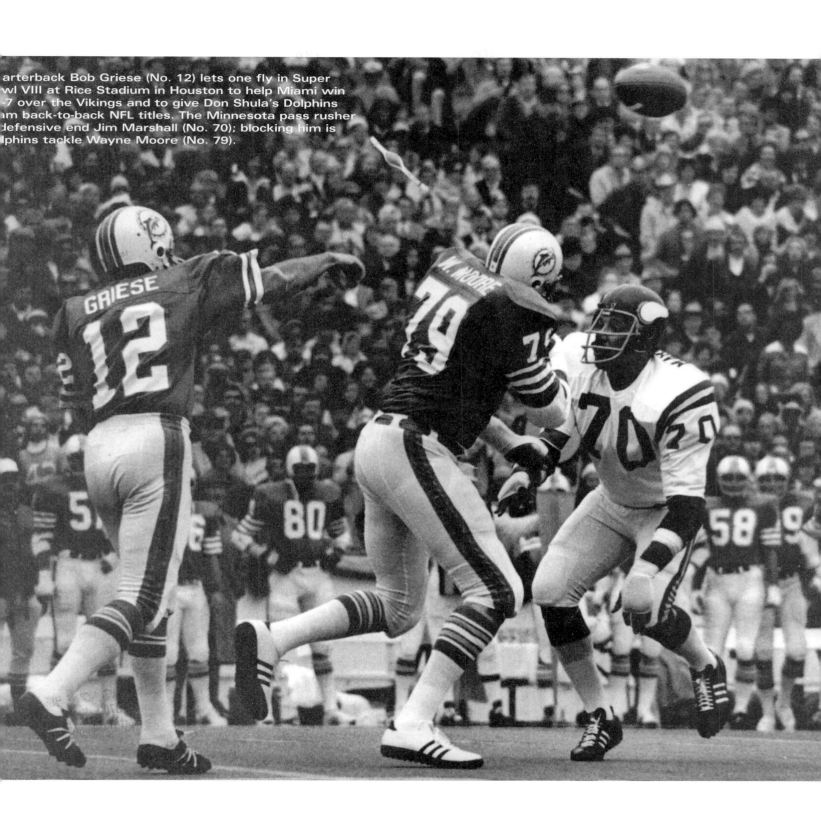

arterback Bob Griese (No. 12) lets one fly in Super
wl VIII at Rice Stadium in Houston to help Miami win
-7 over the Vikings and to give Don Shula's Dolphins
am back-to-back NFL titles. The Minnesota pass rusher
defensive end Jim Marshall (No. 70); blocking him is
lphins tackle Wayne Moore (No. 79).

What really bothered me was having to pose for pictures with the Washington play-ers. I was trying to work myself up to hate those guys, and sharing photos with them rubbed me the wrong way. . . .

Just before the coin toss, [Illinois coach] Pete Elliott came up to me and shouted into my ear above the din, "On their first offensive play, just before the snap, I want every one of our guys to knock one of those Huskies on his ass! Got it? We'll take the penalty. But they'll get the message." I nodded happily. Nothing like a little intimidation to get things off on the right foot.

THOMAS "HOLLYWOOD" HENDERSON'S SPECIAL MEMORIES

Along with their great receivers and ace quarterback, the Cardinals had an excellent offensive line. In my opinion it was the best in all of football: Dan Dierdorf, Tom Banks, Bob Young, and Conrad Dobler. Dobler was the meanest motherf***er out there. He'd stomp on your crotch and spit at you. I can't imagine anybody meaner, except Ray Nitschke when he was drunk.

Ed Jones had a lot of respect for the Cardinals line. After one game in St. Louis he and I were coming out of the locker room and turning into the corridor to go to the bus when I said, "Hey, Too Tall, there's Dan Dierdorf."

Too Tall looked at me. "No," he said, "that's Mr. Dierdorf."

EARL CAMPBELL: HEISMAN IN THE AIR

Our final game of the [1977] regular season was against archrival Texas A&M. As I walked down the tunnel leading to the stadium, [Texas coach Fred] Akers pulled me aside. "Earl, do you want to win that Heisman Trophy?" he asked, getting right in my face.

"Yes sir," I respectfully replied.

"You give me something over a hundred yards and you will win it," he guaranteed me. "You're going to handle the ball 30 times, and each of those needs to be your best of the year. Don't leave the stadium today without everyone singing your praises. You win this game, you'll win the Heisman."

Well, it's like I always say, there's nothing like a little old Heisman Trophy challenge to fire up this country cowboy. I had my biggest day in college football, running for 222 yards and scoring four touchdowns for a 57–28 romp over the Aggies of A&M. The backbreaker came in the fourth quarter, when I swung out on the left side of the field. Quarterback Randy McEachern spotted me and threw a perfect pass. I didn't break stride as the ball landed firmly in my hands. I raced for the end zone as silence fell over A&M's home crowd. The silence was golden.

BART STARR: THE GLAMOUR OF THE PRO GAME

I arrived in Green Bay for the first time on a cloudy day in late June 1956. Unlike the sweltering Alabama summer, the weather there was cool and damp. Sweaters were necessary. "If it's this cold in June," I thought, "what's it going to be like in December?"

At the time, the Packers held their preseason training in Stevens Point, Wisconsin. . . .

We were met at the airport by Tom Miller, a member of the Packers front-office staff, and driven to the Northland Hotel, in the middle of town. Meals were provided directly across the street at the YMCA cafeteria. We worked out at nearby East High School, which was also where the Packers played during the regular season.

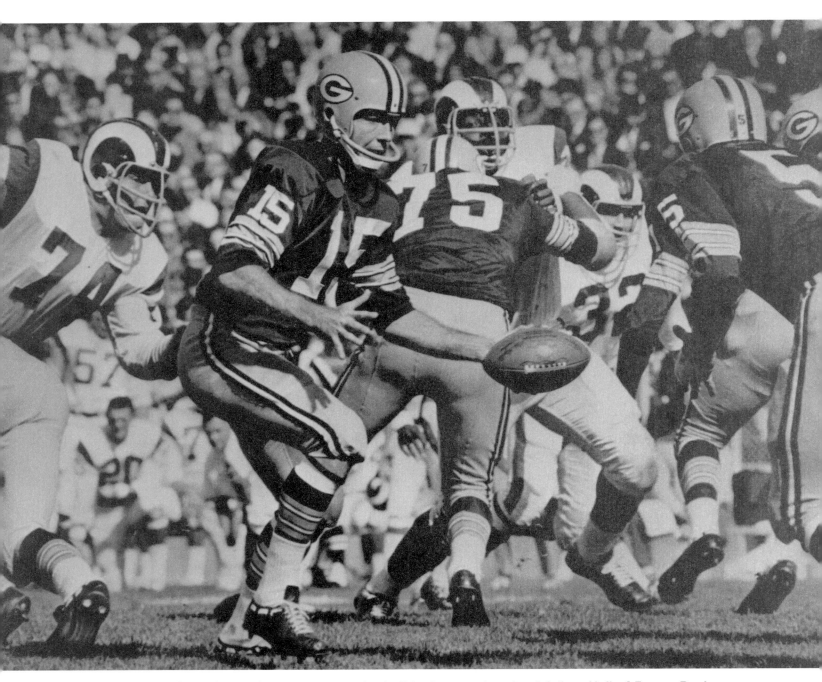

Bart Starr (No. 15) moves to put the ball in the sure hands of fellow Hall of Famer Paul Hornung (No. 5) in a sixties game against the Los Angeles Rams. Starr preceded Hornung into the Pro Football Hall of Fame, inducted in 1977; Hornung had to wait until 1986. Converging on Starr is another Hall of Famer, Rams defensive tackle Merlin Olsen (No. 74). Blocking is still another Hall of Famer, Packers tackle Forrest Gregg (No. 75).

I was shocked when I saw the Packers locker room—33 lockers jammed together in an area no larger than Dad's garage in Montgomery [Alabama]. The Packers offices were located in a red-brick, two-story building next to the Downtowner Motel. The space was so small that the coaches had to enter their offices through a side door.

Our gear was issued to us from a shed near the practice field. The condition of the equipment was far below what I had expected. Gary Knafelc, a wide receiver, recalled, "I had better stuff than that in high school." In fact, while in training camp his rookie year, Gary had his dad send him the pads he used in the College All-Star Game. He wore them the entire season.

JOE NAMATH: SUPER BOWL III

Three days before the game, after I got my right knee drained again and had some pain reliever shot into my left knee for the tendon there that's always inflamed, I went down to Miami Springs Villas to receive an award from the Touchdown Club....

"We're going to win Sunday," I told the people at the Touchdown Club dinner. "I'll guarantee you. . . ."

I study football, and I understand it—well, I understand some of it—and when I say we're a better football team, you can go to sleep on that. I know the better football team doesn't always win, but when you've got the better team plus 18 points— the price had gone up a point by then; there must've been a lot of stupid people running to the bookmakers—it's like stealing. . . .

I just prayed that the Colts would blitz us. If they did, I figured they were dead. Our backs are just the best there are at picking up a blitz. Matt Snell and Bill Mathis are fantastic, and Emerson Boozer keeps getting better and better, both [at] blocking and reading defenses. And our ends, Don Maynard and George Sauer and Pete

Lammons, can smell a blitz a mile away. They've got a whole bunch of little signals to change their patterns, like, if Maynard winks at me, he means he's going to run an I pattern. In the 1968 season we handled the blitz like crazy. Against Miami, we completed five touchdown passes, and all five came against the blitz. Anybody that's ever played in the American Football League will tell you not to blitz against New York. Of course, the Colts didn't know that.

I don't want to take anything away from the Colts. Taking the world championship is enough. They're a helluva football team. [Tom] Matte's a great runner, and they hit hard, and they play clean, tough football. But, just like I'd been saying all along and everybody'd been laughing, the Jets are a great football team, too. People say Sauer and Maynard and Lammons are good, and that's not half enough to describe them. And our defense was just beyond belief. The people who came to the Super Bowl saw a great defensive team, but it wasn't the Colts.

> "I was born with a strong throwing arm. Me and both my brothers, Gary and Craig, had very strong arms. Some families inherit intelligence, others get good looks; we got right arms."
>
> —TERRY BRADSHAW

RAY NITSCHKE: MIDDLE LINEBACKING

A year or two before I got [to the Packers], the pro teams had changed from a five-man line to a four-man line. This gave the middle linebacker more responsibility. He had to be big enough to stop the run, but quick enough to cover short receivers.

Green Bay cornerback Herb Adderley (No. 26) returns an interception in the 1961 NFL title game against the Giants. A first-round draft pick that year from Michigan State, he stayed with the Packers through 1969, then spent his last three years in the NFL with the Dallas Cowboys. An All-Pro and Pro Bowl attendee five times, he was also a great kickoff returner (more than 3,000 yards in his 12-year career) and had 48 career interceptions. He was inducted into the Pro Football of Fame in 1980. No. 14 on New York is quarterback Y. A. Tittle, whose pass Adderley picked off.

Green Bay middle linebacker Ray Nitschke (No. 66) has his sights set on scrambling Bears quarterback Rudy Bukich (No. 10) in a 1965 game at Lambeau Field. Another Green Bay great also has his eyes riveted on Bukich, defensive end Willie Davis (No. 87). The rivalry between the Bears and Packers goes all the way back to 1921, the second year of the NFL's existence. The Bears lost this game, then beat the Pack later down in Chicago, but Green Bay went on to win the NFL championship that year.

In college ball, you were primarily interested in stopping the run because there wasn't so much passing. With the pros, the linebacker's responsibility for defending against the pass was much greater.

I knew the Packers hadn't done too well the season before. In fact, before I reported to training camp, [Lisle] Blackbourn had been fired, and Ray "Scooter" McLean was coach. But it was a professional team, regardless of its won-lost record, and it was something for a young guy who'd been a fan to know he was going to be on the same squad as people like Jim Ringo, Bill Forester, Dave Hanner, and Bill Howton—not to mention a 235-pound player named Tom Bettis, who was starting his third season. Bettis was the one I had to beat out if I wanted to be a first-string middle linebacker, which was exactly what I planned to be.

WEIGHING LES BINGAMAN

In his book *Heart of a Lion*, Bob St. John told this story about one of the great behemoths of the earlier days of the NFL:

> An annual game in the Detroit Lions training camp in
> Ypsilanti, Michigan, was guessing the weight of gigantic
> middle guard Les Bingaman. The estimates usually ran
> that he carried anywhere from 300 to 400 pounds over
> his 6'3" frame. There were no scales in training camp
> equipped to weigh such a man. [Bobby] Layne said they
> once used two scales, having Les put a foot on each one,
> but they both went over 200 and there was some question

as to their accuracy. Bobby also liked to tell the story about the time it was decided, once and for all, to determine what his good friend actually weighed. They located a scale at a nearby Farm Bureau that would register up to 400 pounds and decided to try it out.

"The whole thing started when [head coach] Buddy Parker and [defensive coach] Buster Ramsey got into an argument over how much Slim weighed and made a bet," said Layne. "Slim had sat down one day to tie his shoe and the bench collapsed under him. Buddy said he must weigh 400 pounds and Buster said it was closer to 330. So Buddy bet him a steak that Slim was closer to 400 than 300.

"We went to the Farm Bureau and Slim got on a scale they used for weighing bags of grain. He tipped the scales to exactly 349 pounds. Buddy lost by eight ounces."

TERRY BRADSHAW: CALLING HIS OWN PLAYS

To really be in charge, you've got to call your own plays. In my opinion, any quarterback who calls his plays automatically has it all over one who doesn't. It's up to the quarterback in charge to distribute the football to the right players and make certain everybody gets a piece of the action. And when something is not going right, the quarterback who calls his own plays doesn't have to look over to the bench and hope the coach senses it.

Terry Bradshaw (No. 12) was a ball carrier to contend with when he had to be, evidenced here as he steps out in Super Bowl X. The 6'3", 215-pound quarterback led the Steelers to four Super Bowl victories in the seventies. During his 14-year career in Pittsburgh, Bradshaw carried the ball for 32 touchdowns to complement the 212 passes he threw for TDs.

Calling my plays gave me a better feel for the tempo of the game. If Franco's [fullback Franco Harris] hot, I call his number. If [wide receiver Lynn] Swann's hot, I go right back to him. If I need to go deep to [wide receiver John] Stallworth, I do it. All instinctively.

You can't be instinctive when you're waiting for the play to come in from the bench.

BO JACKSON: WATCHING OUT FOR ONESELF

There are plenty of vultures who are looking to take advantage of athletes. Some of them are white, and some are black. Most of the athletes who get taken advantage of are black. Maybe 95 percent of us grew up with nothing, and so, when somebody says to us, "Hey, here's $500, there's $1,000 to hold you over, let me know if you need more, and, oh yeah, when you're ready to turn pro, I'll get you the best deal," we get sucked in, too many of us. They con you, and they fool you, and they get you locked in.

It's bad enough when it's white guys taking advantage of black athletes, but to me, it's even worse when black guys do it.

"You should let a brother handle your business."

"Where'd you go to school, brother?"

"Well, I didn't exactly finish."

"You think I'm gonna allow somebody who didn't finish college to handle my money? Man, get a real life! Stop mooching off people."

I had that conversation more than once.

LYLE ALZADO ON ART SHELL

When you've been a street fighter, sometimes you'll resort to old tactics when you get frustrated. On the field, Art Shell—the Raiders' 295-pound left tackle—is one of the meanest, vilest guys I ever played against. He'll cuss me, grab me, spit in my face, and I'll punch him, spit in his face, and cuss him right back. I might say something about his mother and father, too, but I don't hate the guy, I respect him. People always ask me what it's like to play against Art Shell, but the only way I can describe it is to ask them: "Have you ever been attacked by wild dogs?"

"Pro football gave me a great sense of perspective to enter politics. I'd already been booed, cheered, cut, sold, traded, and hung in effigy."

—JACK KEMP

WE JUST CAN'T HAVE THIS KIND OF THING, CONRAD

There was a little chitchat between us before [NFL commissioner Pete] Rozelle began. "Well, Conrad [Dobler], there have been a few complaints about you. But I'm not going to get into that myself. I'm going to call in Art McNally, our director of officials."

That was Rozelle's way of telling me that, while the final decision on punishment would be his, he wasn't going to get into a debate over it with me. That was Art McNally's job. . . .

The three of us then headed for Rozelle's private screening room. With the commissioner walking on one side of me and McNally on the other, I felt like a defendant being led into court—the only thing missing were the handcuffs. . . .

Conrad Dobler (left) of the St. Louis Cardinals blocks a charging George Martin of the Giants during the fourth quarter of a 1977 game in East Rutherford, New Jersey. *Photo courtesy of AP/Wide World Photos.*

The big eye in the sky had caught everything: the cheap shot I gave [A. J.] Duhe, the fight with [Bob] Matheson and [Kim] Bokamper, the shove I gave [Alvin] Wyatt. (McNally said the only reason I wasn't suspended for pushing the referee was that he pushed me first, and it was only natural for me to respond the way I did.) With the final scene from the Miami game, I figured the show was over.

Little did I know it was only the beginning. . . .

The league office actually had gone through the films of every game I'd ever played in to splice together samples of the dirty tactics I had used through the first six years of my career. There were scenes of me punching guys, hitting them under the chin, hitting them out of bounds, hitting them in the knees, elbowing them in the throat, leg-whipping (a form of tripping), kicking, kneeing, stepping on face masks (with the faces still behind them), piling on, and, of course, holding. They had missed shots of me biting and eye-gouging, but I assume this was only because the photographers didn't use their zoom lenses.

With each scene, I sank lower and lower into my chair—to the point where I could barely see the screen over the seat back in front of me. My shirt was soaked with sweat. Except for the whir of the projector, there was dead silence in the room as McNally ran the film back and forth, back and forth. . . .

After the lights came on, Rozelle said, "We just can't have this sort of thing in the NFL, Conrad."

THOMAS "HOLLYWOOD" HENDERSON: FIRST IMPRESSIONS

After a couple of weeks of rookie camp, all the regulars came in. I had been the most talented player in camp, the top draft choice, the loudest, the most notable. All of a sudden, I died. Camp changed.

Here by my side were Lee Roy Jordan and D. D. Lewis and Dave Edwards, the Cowboys linebackers. I was watching Ed "Too Tall" Jones and Jethro Pugh and Harvey Martin and Larry Cole work on the line. In the defensive backfield there was Mel Renfro and Cornell Green and Cliff Harris and Charlie Waters. Across the line of the offense there were these guys I'd seen on TV: Roger Staubach, Drew Pearson, Jean Fugett. At center was John Fitzgerald, next to him Blaine Nye, Ralph Neely, John Niland, Rayfield Wright. Billy Joe Dupree at tight end, running backs Robert Newhouse and Doug Dennison. I was watching like a kid for a second as they went through their paces.

The first thing I noticed was the sound. There is this very special sound when guys hit each other: it's clean and brutal, grunts and crashing as plastic hits plastic and man hits man. There's nothing like it in real life; you don't hear this sound unless you're right down there next to it, inside it. In college I was usually the one making that sound, doling it out. Maybe once every couple of minutes I'd hear it from somebody else. The first set of downs in our first contact scrimmage I heard that sound five or six times *every play.* Somebody was either hitting or getting hit, accepting a hit or dishing it out for real. I was impressed.

ART DONOVAN: ON QUARTERBACKS

Now I'm not going to tell you that when I played, from 1950 through 1961, every team was all one big, happy family, because I'm not going to bullshit you. We had our share of rats on the team. But, by and large, most of us hung around together, even with the guys on the other team. I love the way they make Jim McMahon out to be football's "rebel without a cause." It's as if they've never heard of a guy who likes beer before. Then again, maybe they haven't.

One of the game's greatest passers, Sonny Jurgensen fades back for the Redskins in a 1968 game. A Philadelphia Eagle from 1957 through 1963, he joined Washington in 1964 to begin an 11-year career there. The Duke alum threw for more than 3,000 yards in three of those seasons; he also passed for more than 400 yards in five games and more than 300 in 25 games.

Otto Graham, a tailback in his college days at Northwestern, was converted to a T-formation quarterback in the pros, where he excelled for 10 years (1946–1955). The first four were with the Cleveland Browns in the AAFC, the last six with the Browns in the NFL. During those 10 years he led Cleveland to 10 division or league titles, and was All-League himself in 9 of them.

McMahon is only following in the footsteps of some of the flightiest quarter-backs to ever play the game. Nut jobs like Norm Van Brocklin, Sonny Jurgensen, Otto Graham, Charlie Conerly, Joe Namath, Don Meredith, and Kenny Stabler spring to mind. I'm sure there are more. But there is just one man who rises head and shoulders above the rest when it comes to setting the standard for good times, on and off the field.

That man, of course, was one Robert Layne, a legend in his spare time.

MIKE DITKA: NEGOTIATING WITH GEORGE HALAS

One of my favorite stories is about Ed O'Bradovich negotiating with him. Ed made up his mind that he had to have a certain amount of money. He said he was worth a raise of $4,000. The old man told him how bad he'd played and how much money the Bears were losing. Ed lowered it to $3,000. Then Halas would accuse Ed of whoring around and hanging around with the wrong crowd and not doing his calisthenics properly. Ed lowered it to $2,000. Halas would go on and get it down in Ed's mind to $1,000. By the time they were through, Ed stood up and said, "Hey Coach, let me give you a check for $500."

DICK BUTKUS: PARTYING

I got my first hint that maybe I was beginning to be accepted by some of the older players. One day, [Ed] O'Bradovich came over to me on the practice field and said that if I was a good boy, I might be invited to Bob Wetoska's birthday party. . . .

The beer begins to flow immediately, and pretty soon someone suggests a drinking contest among the rookies. . . .

[Mike] Ditka wraps his head with a bandanna and declares himself the referee. A table is cleared and two large glasses of beer are set down. Brian [Piccolo] and I face off on either side of the table. Ditka slaps his big mitts, signaling the start, and I drain my glass before Brian barely has his to his lips. Applause and hoots and hollers from the defense rock the saloon, and the gambling begins. [Richie] Petitbon and O.B. [Ed O'Bradovich] bankroll the effort, and pretty soon I am beating everyone the offense throws against me.

After about an hour of this, I am getting pretty shitfaced. But I'm still functioning. Then someone yells, "Hey! We gotta get to our meeting! It's almost 7:00!" Chairs scrape back as everyone gets up to leave. Everyone except Doug Atkins. He is standing at the door with a bottle of Wild Turkey, informing us that nobody is going anywhere. As big as some of us were, Doug Atkins was in a league by himself. I never saw anybody like Atkins. *Nobody* ever saw anybody like Atkins: 6'8", 275 pounds, and not enough fat on him to cook an egg. On top of that, he was not your typical gentle giant. Dougie's exploits were legend in pro football camps from Baltimore to Oakland.

There we were, all gathered around the door, pleading, "C'mon, Doug, don't be like that," and, "Gee, Dougie, we don't wanna get in trouble on our last day in camp."

But Doug was resolute. "We ain't gonna go to no damned meeting. I'm tired of this bullshit." Then he takes another jolt of Wild Turkey and stares at all of us. Finally someone promises him that we will come back right after the meeting, so Doug says, "Well, OK then. But first everyone has to take a swig of this Wild Turkey."

So we all line up and take our medicine, which does not sit all that well on top of a couple of gallons of beer. I jump in my Buick Riviera and fly to the local hall

Dallas defensive end Ed "Too Tall" Jones (No. 72) applies a painful pat on the cheek to Broncos quarterback Norris Weese in Super Bowl XII. It was but one indignity the Cowboys heaped on Denver that January afternoon in 1978, defeating them 27–10 to take the NFL championship. The 6'9" Jones, from Tennessee State, was a defensive standout for the Cowboys from 1974 through 1978, then took 1979 off to test his skills as a professional boxer. He returned to the football field in 1980 and played again for the Cowboys for most of the decade. No. 79 for Dallas is defensive end Harvey Martin.

where we held our team meetings. As I arrive at the building, I neglect to hit the brakes in a timely manner, and the car stops halfway up the stairs leading to the front door. I'm lucky I don't kill anyone. . . .

That was the first of many team parties.

> "Everyone has some fear. A man who has no fear belongs in a mental institution. Or on special teams."
>
> —WALT MICHAELS, WHILE HEAD COACH OF THE NEW YORK JETS

TERRY BRADSHAW: COMING TO THE STEEL CITY

Pittsburgh. Pray tell, how did I get there in the first place? Pittsburgh. So foreign to me as a college student at Louisiana Tech in 1970 that upon being drafted by the Steelers, I had to race to the encyclopedia and look up its location. I opened the book to a picture of this northeastern, industrial city and tried, in vain, to imagine myself, a country boy from Louisiana, among all those smokestacks. Pittsburgh. A city with a 40-year history of losing pro football teams. A hard-nosed, blue-collar, shot-and-a-beer town without much of an appetite for raw, rookie quarterbacks. A city and a team that had once discarded the great Johnny Unitas. Pittsburgh. Home of the Steelers, a team with the ugliest uniforms I had seen since I wore the red and black colors of Oak Terrace Junior High in Shreveport.

Pittsburgh. Cold and dark and frightening to a boy from the sunny South, who had dreamed since the age of seven of playing quarterback in the NFL.

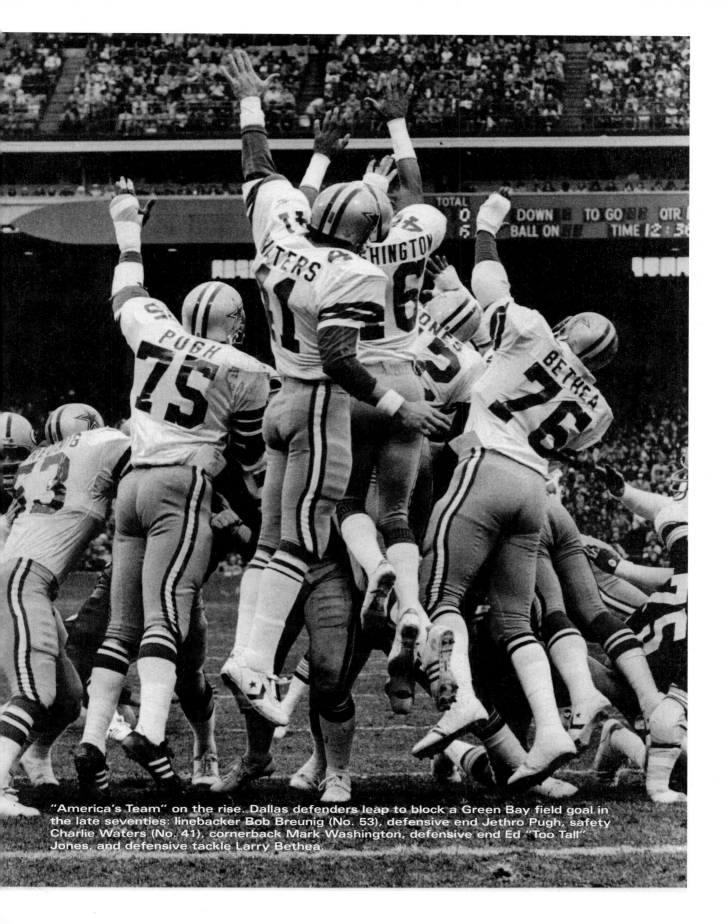

"America's Team" on the rise. Dallas defenders leap to block a Green Bay field goal in the late seventies: linebacker Bob Breunig (No. 53), defensive end Jethro Pugh, safety Charlie Waters (No. 41), cornerback Mark Washington, defensive end Ed "Too Tall" Jones, and defensive tackle Larry Bethea.

KEN STABLER: LOVE THAT TRAINING CAMP

Some of my most vivid memories are of training camps. Although many players have compared life in a National Football League training camp to being in a Turkish prison, I loved it.

The Oakland Raiders of my day trained in the long-sucking heat of Santa Rosa, California, where the sweat poured like rain for eight weeks. The workouts were scheduled for 90 minutes in the morning and 90 minutes in the afternoon. But I'd like to have an Al Davis pinkie ring for every workout that lasted over two hours. We got so much conditioning in during practice, we didn't have to do the extra running that other teams did. Which was fine—we weren't entering any marathons.

But we worked like hell in practice and tried to keep from snoring like hell in meetings: 90 minutes in the afternoon, 90 more in the evening. The meetings were so boring they made leaf-raking seem like an exciting occupation. I can understand why so many players hated training camp.

ROCKY BLEIER: A CURIOUS TRADITION

The arrival of the veterans [to training camp] also meant the resumption of a fine old Steelers tradition . . . happy hour before dinner. During two-a-day practices, we were off the field at 4:30, with dinner scheduled for 6:00. So, if you showered in about a minute and 15 seconds, dressed on the way to the parking lot, and drove the country roads of Latrobe like Jackie Stewart at Monte Carlo, you'd have exactly one hour of heaven in a little pub called the Nineteenth Hole.

It was Paul Martha, a defensive back and off-season attorney, who first explained it to me. He said, "Bleier, I like you. You're a good kid. You worked hard out there today, and I think it's time you replaced some of your natural body fluids.

Besides, the biggest hell-raisers in the NFL have consistently come from Notre Dame—great names like Paul Hornung, Monty Stickles, Myron Pottios, Mike Lind. I'd like to see you uphold that tradition. I never met a man from Notre Dame who couldn't drink beer and drink it well, in large quantities. I'm betting on you this afternoon at the Nineteenth Hole."

The veterans would bet each other which rookie could drink the most beer. . . .

So I dutifully drank every beer he placed in front of me that first evening, which was 13. (Another night, a big rookie tackle named Ernie Ruple of Arkansas drank that many shots of whiskey, and favored us with a like number of "sooooooooooooooooey pig" hog calls before passing out in a contest with Ben McGee.) I was also assigned to take the little aluminum ring-top from every veterans' beer can and fasten them into a chain. They cut my fingers a thousand different ways, but I was too drunk to care.

BORROWING A LINE FROM BABE RUTH

From the book *Blanda: Alive and Kicking*, a fascinating dialogue that may even have taken place:

Houston sports editor: "What? You're bringing me another picture of George Blanda? Do you realize that this paper has run more pictures of Blanda than it has of President Eisenhower?"

Oiler publicity man Jack Scott: "That's because Blanda is having a better year."

Pro football's grand old man, George Blanda, calls the signals for the Raiders in the early seventies. Blanda, hailing from the University of Kentucky, joined the Chicago Bears in 1949; 27 years later, at age 48, he ended his NFL career as an Oakland Raider. He played quarterback and place kicked for the Bears for 10 years, joined the Houston Oilers for seven years, and played for the Raiders nine years. When he retired, he had accounted for 2,002 points, then an NFL record, and he had tied or set 15 other NFL marks.

JIM BROWN: TECHNIQUE

I would always look for the least amount of resistance, and if that meant not getting touched, that was perfectly cool. If I had a choice of running around you, or over you, I'd go around you. I wanted the yards, not to prove my manhood.

Now, if I couldn't run around you, then we'd have to deal. Then I wanted to hit you as hard as you hit me. No, I wanted to hit you harder. I wanted your nose stinging; bleeding was OK, too. I wanted you flinching and demoralized. The next time you saw me coming, I wanted you to say, oh shit.

"He's a perfectionist. If he was married to Raquel Welch, he'd expect her to cook."

—DON MEREDITH ON TOM LANDRY

TERRY BRADSHAW: REMEMBERING THE IMMACULATE RECEPTION, 1972

When you get knocked to the ground on a football field and can't see the action, you listen carefully for telltale sounds. You learn to read those noises the way an Indian reads bear tracks. There's a good roar and a bad roar.

I was on my back and couldn't see anything but gray sky overhead, green artificial turf, and black and silver uniforms on top of me. The ball was somewhere on the way toward [John] Fuqua—I thought—because as I unloaded it, I thought I saw a No. 33 in the middle of the field. So I turned up my hearing to listen for a clue as to what had happened.

Of all the roars I have ever heard, there's never been one to compare to that one. As I picked my head up off the turf, knowing instinctively that all but a few seconds had expired on the game clock, I had the feeling something wonderful had happened. The fans were going nuts. And as I jumped up, I saw something truly miraculous: Franco [Harris] crossing the goal line and going into the end zone. . . .

Fans streamed onto the field, some of them mobbing me. I realized we had won, but I still didn't know how. "This is unbelievable! Unbelievable!" I said. "Somebody tell me. What happened?"

They just kept hollering, "You did it, you did it."

And I kept asking, "Did what? Somebody please tell me!"

RAY NITSCHKE: INJURIES

On the next play, Tom Watkins was trying to block me, and I hit his helmet a good crack with my forearm. I felt something snap, and it wasn't Tom's neck.

"My arm's broken, guys," I said back in the huddle. "I'm taking myself out."

"Oh, no you aren't, Nitschke," Dan Currie said. "Wait until this series is over."

So I stayed in, trying not to let the Lions know I was hurt. But I wasn't going to hit anybody with that arm. It was numb. There was no strength left in it. But even with only one arm to use, I got in on the next couple of plays. In fact, in one of them I got in far enough so I got my nose broken, too.

ART DONOVAN: INJURIES

Christ, when [Wilbur] "Weeb" Ewbank was coaching the Colts, he had a special squad stationed along our sideline ready to run onto the field and pull injured guys off so we didn't have to waste a timeout. They weren't instructed to handle the wounded with prenatal care, either. There were three guys in particular Weeb liked

Franco Harris (No. 32) carries the ball for the Steelers against the Vikings in Super Bowl IX. A product of Penn State, Harris was Pittsburgh's number one pick in the 1972 NFL draft, playing for them through the 1983 season; he finished his NFL career with a year playing for the Seattle Seahawks. In this title game, which the Steelers won 16–6, Harris set Super Bowl records with 34 carries for 158 yards (since broken) and was named the game's MVP. Chasing him is Minnesota defensive end Alan Page (No. 88).

The Green Bay sweep of the Lombardi era is captured here in all its glory. Fullback Jim Taylor carries after a handoff from Bart Starr; pulling to block for him are guards Jerry Kramer (No. 64) and Fuzzy Thurston (No. 63). Between Starr (No. 15) and Taylor, coach Vince Lombardi can be seen on the sideline.

to use—Don Shula, Carl Taseff, and Bert Rechichar—because they were defensive backs and they were fast. Unless you had a broken tibia sticking out through your uniform, they'd be scurrying in there and dragging you off by your feet, arms, head, anything, usually leaving a trail of blood and a stadium of echoing howls.

Weeb would deny this; he does to this day. But he's bullshitting.

DON'T LET A LITTLE PAIN STOP YOU, HOLLYWOOD

Two Cowboys physicians came into the locker room. One said, "How are you feeling?"

"Well, Doc," I [Thomas "Hollywood" Henderson] moaned, "right here, Doc."

He touched it, and I jumped. It was already inflamed. That quickly. The muscle on my hip was three times its normal size. "I'm hurt."

"Do you think you can play?"

"No, man, I can't play, man. I can't walk."

"Well, let me see what we can do."

I got up on the trainer's table and he felt around and found the spot. "Yeah," I groaned, "that's exactly where I got hit, Doc." I couldn't stop moaning and groaning.

One doctor took this needle and shot me right there full of Xylocaine. In 20 seconds the pain went away. All the way away. Then he injected me again with more Xylocaine in the general area. It felt like from rib cage out I had this giant piece of dead skin. There was no feeling at all.

The trainer gave me two pills. "What are these?"

"Oh, just codeine."

"Codeine?"

"Codeine IVs. We have IIIs and IVs, and we give IVs when you're hurting."

I took the two codeines, and the doctor pulled out another needle. "What's happening, man?" I said. "How many times you going to shoot me up here?"

"It's just cortisone. It's all right. This is part of the treatment. This will help the area on your bone where you got hit heal more quickly."

They put a big doughnut pad on my hip for protection. It stuck out six or eight inches and I couldn't feel it, but it seemed to me like two feet of me was hanging off the side. Then coach [Mike] Ditka came in the training room.

"Henderson, how are you feeling?"

"Well, I don't feel nothing." I was a little amazed.

He looked at me. "We're going to run the reverse."

I wasn't sure I was there. "I don't know if I can."

I got up off the table, bent to the left, bent to the right. I didn't feel a damn thing. No pain, no discomfort, no nothing.

Coach [Jerry] Tubbs came in for a look-see. He looked at coach Ditka and at me and asked the classic football question, the only question anyone's really interested in.

"Can you go?"

That's professional football in a phrase. If you can't go, go see the doctor until you can. If you can, then let's go.

A guy would rather hobble out with all kinds of stuff busted up inside than tell a coach he can't go, 'cause if you can't go now, someone else can. And if you can't go now, maybe you can't go next game. And if you can't go then, what can you do? Why are you here? To go. So let's go.

I told Ditka, "Yeah, I think I can run that sucker."

"John Riggins, like Joe Namath, is an enigma
wrapped in a bandage."

—SPORTSWRITER AND AUTHOR
LARRY MERCHANT

THE ICE BOWL: BART STARR REMEMBERS

Coach Vince Lombardi prohibited us from wearing an excessive amount of under-clothing because he believed it restricted our movement. But even he wore long underwear on that day. Every player would have welcomed the skintight gloves so prevalent now. Had they been available, I might have avoided frostbite. I still shiver when I hear the words *Ice Bowl.*

Imagine how difficult it was to ignore the elements and concentrate on the most important play in Packers history. With 16 seconds remaining in the 1967 NFL championship game, I called our final timeout. We had possession of the ball two feet from the Dallas goal line. The Cowboys led 17–14, but we were in the driver's seat.

My concern about the icy turf prompted me to ask Jerry Kramer, our All-Pro right guard, "Can you get your footing for a wedge play?"

"Hell, yes!" he confidently shot back through the roar of the crowd.

I turned and jogged to the sideline to plot strategy with coach Lombardi. A field goal would have tied the game and forced a sudden-death overtime. But it never crossed his mind . . . the time to win was now.

THE ICE BOWL: RAY NITSCHKE REMEMBERS

[Chuck] Mercein didn't score. But he got us down in Dallas territory. Now we had a chance for a field goal, and that would send the game into sudden-death overtime.

One of professional football's most famous photographs: the historic quarterback sneak by the Packers' Bart Starr (No. 15) in the 1967 NFL championship game against the Cowboys—a game better known as the "Ice Bowl." At Lambeau Field in Green Bay, the temperature was –13°F with 15 mile-an-hour winds. The game was finally decided on this touchdown play with 13 seconds remaining. The final: Green Bay 21, Dallas 17. On the ground is guard Jerry Kramer (No. 64), who drove the key block into Dallas defensive tackle Jethro Pugh (No. 75).

Considering how cold my feet were, staying out there to play in overtime didn't sound like too great an idea. But it would be better than losing.

[Bart] Starr still had 90 seconds to go, though. We had the ball on their 30. There was a time when he could have handed the ball to [Jim] Taylor, and Jim would have put his head down and defied anybody in a Cowboys uniform to stop him. There was a time when Bart could have given the ball to [Paul] Hornung, and Paul would have smelled all that winner's money and would have slipped past tacklers and been on his way. But Taylor was in New Orleans, and Hornung was up in the stands without his shoulder pads. So Starr had to think of some other way to win. . . .

He looked over at Lombardi. There might be time for only one play. A field goal was almost sure from here, and three points would tie the game. Then we could take our time going out there and making sure we scored first in overtime. Sending Don Chandler and the kicking team in was the safe and sensible thing to do. The coach believed in conservative football. He didn't believe in taking a chance of not coming away with some points in a situation like that, and this was the biggest game of his career.

Afterward, Lombardi said he'd taken pity on all those freezing people in the stands and decided to go for broke so the game would end, one way or another. You can believe that if you want to. But I think he kept Chandler on the sidelines and gave Starr one last chance to win the game to show his love and respect for the players.

EARL CAMPBELL MEETS JACK TATUM

One run I do take pride in was against the Oakland Raiders in 1979. I have heard sportscasters call it my "greatest hit." We drove the ball all the way down inside the Raiders' 10-yard line. [Dan] Pastorini handed me the ball, and I went straight ahead.

Jack Tatum, the most vicious tackler in the league, came up and slammed his helmet into my chest. I staggered back a step, but managed to twist and keep my momentum going into the end zone. Pastorini said later that the collision was so violent it sounded like a train wreck. As I lay in the end zone looking back at Tatum through my helmet, I thought, "I just beat the best."

DICK BUTKUS: PALOOKAVILLE

[One] memory, in particular, is funny. Our second exhibition game was against the Redskins in Memorial Stadium. In the middle of the second quarter, I was kneed in the head while tackling the running back. The next thing I know, I'm sitting on the sideline, looking up and down the bench. There's Rosey Taylor, O.B. [Ed O'Bradovich], [Doug] Atkins, and all the rest. Then [defensive coach George] Allen comes down, his clipboard under his arm, and he leans over and looks into my eyes and says something like:

"You OK, Dick? You ready to go?"

So I say, "Am I OK? Yeah, I'm OK. Let's go."

Then Allen says, "What's the score?"

I look at him like maybe he's drunk, which would have been a first, and I say, "You're asking me what the score is? We haven't even started yet."

Then I see that some of the guys are smiling, and I look back at George and ask, "Have we?"

George says, "Just sit there and take it easy."

Then it occurs to me that I'm all dirty and sweaty, so I look on the field and of course the game is going on. Then I look at the scoreboard. It's the beginning of the fourth quarter. I'd been out to lunch for more than half the game. Well, my eyes must have looked OK because Allen sent me in soon after that.

JIM BROWN: AN UNPLEASANT MEMORY

Hard men. Not a lot of cash. It made the old NFL a primitive place. I accepted the standard rough stuff, knew it was part of my sport. Still, the first time I carried the ball against the Giants, I knew something was *up.* We used to wear those two-bar masks; from the bottom of the nose to just above the eyebrow was exposed. As I was going down my first carry, a guy stuck his hand inside my helmet and scraped my eyes. On the next carry, my eye got hit by a forearm. As the first half went on, I guess the Giants got pretty blatant. Rosey Grier, their huge defensive end, started screaming at his own teammates: *"What the hell are you doing that for?"*

Me and Rosey were real friends, and the Giants knew it. I don't believe they sent him that morning's memo.

"The thing is that by the time I quit playing, I was too old to be starting out as a coach."

—George Blanda

CLIFF HARRIS ON A ROLE MODEL

We all have our heroes. Let me tell you about Lee Roy Jordan. When I was growing up in Arkansas, I watched him play for the University of Alabama, and I thought, he is the perfect college football player. If I could ever play as well as him, I'd be truly satisfied.

Lee Roy was a very intense, very intelligent guy. He was the leader of the Doomsday Defense, the guy that took you under his wing. We had somewhat similar backgrounds—he came from a small, rural farm town in Alabama—and he helped me enormously to understand how the total system worked.

High-flying Cliff Harris (No. 43) in a game against the New Orleans Saints in the seventies. Harris carried the ball for Dallas on kick returns (when he retired after the 1979 season he was the Cowboys second all-time kickoff returner, with 1,622 yards) or when he intercepted a pass playing in the defensive backfield (for which he earned invitations to six Pro Bowls).

I remember one play in particular. We were playing Philadelphia, and it was fourth and goal on about the 1. I was lined up as a linebacker, along with Lee Roy.

An Eagle running back tried to jump over the line of scrimmage, and Lee Roy and I met him head on at the line of scrimmage and drove him back. We won the game with just seconds left. If ever I could have a picture of my playing days, that would have been the picture, the one I'd feature in my scrapbook. Because that, to me, was the culmination of all my football playing years. From the time I was a kid I'd dreamed of it, and there I was on the field right alongside someone who was my hero, making the play of the day.

213

THE VIKINGS OF '61: FRAN TARKENTON AND JIM KLOBUCHAR REMEMBER

In their original trappings, the Vikings were not so much a team as a loosely maintained wildlife preserve.

Their first-year roster was the post office wall of the National Football League. The Vikings were the only team in pro football whose press book compilers seriously considered including fingerprints. Some of the heroic renegades and aging desperadoes of football found lodgings with the 1961 Vikings. Many of them were men who had once played honorably, but had sinned by getting old, rebellious, or fat. None of these qualities underwent any substantial change when they got to Minnesota.

THE PACK IN '58: RAY NITSCHKE REMEMBERS

In 1958 Lambeau Field held only thirty-six thousand. . . . It started as a horseshoe and now it's a bowl. All around the league, the size of the stadiums has increased,

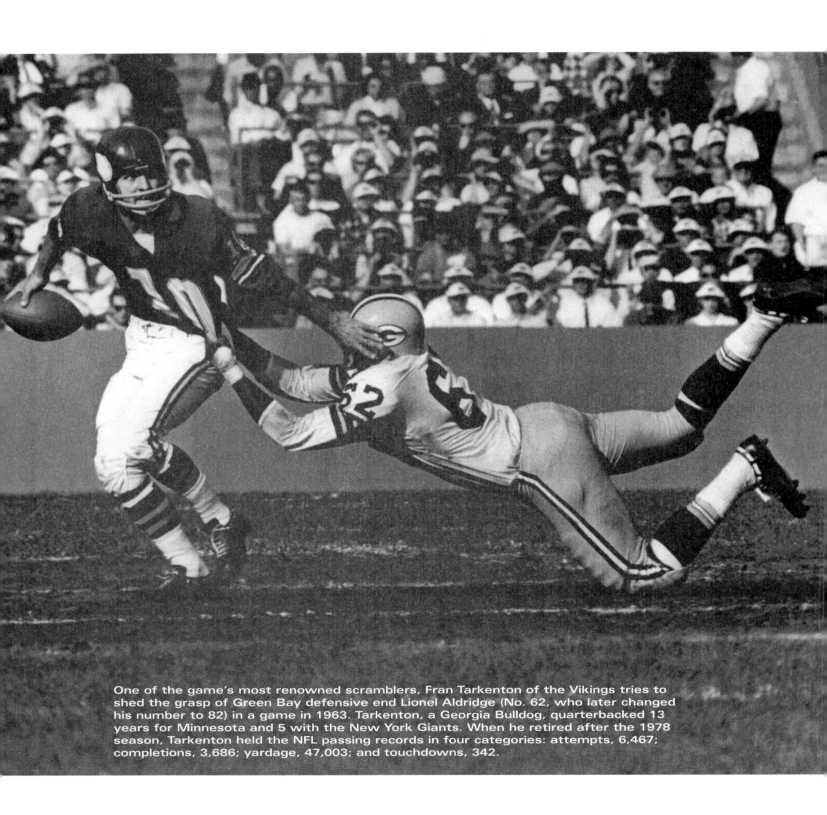

One of the game's most renowned scramblers, Fran Tarkenton of the Vikings tries to shed the grasp of Green Bay defensive end Lionel Aldridge (No. 62, who later changed his number to 82) in a game in 1963. Tarkenton, a Georgia Bulldog, quarterbacked 13 years for Minnesota and 5 with the New York Giants. When he retired after the 1978 season, Tarkenton held the NFL passing records in four categories: attempts, 6,467; completions, 3,686; yardage, 47,003; and touchdowns, 342.

and every year there are more people at the games. There are other differences, too. In 1958 we stayed at nice enough places when we were on the road. But there were hotels that didn't want our business. They preferred not to be associated with football players. We were looked on as a rough, tough bunch of brutes. . . .

In 1958 you could take off your helmet and put on regular clothes and nobody knew you. Today, it's amazing how often people recognize you on the street. It's like you were a movie star. With my bald head and horn-rim glasses—not to mention when I put in my front teeth after the game—I look a lot different away from the stadium, but people seem to know me just the same.

ON THE FIELD WITH BOBBY LAYNE

Author Bob St. John remembered this about the quarterback who was as famous for his off-field behavior as his on-field greatness:

> All-Pro tackle Lou Creekmur agreed. "If you missed a block, Bobby made sure everybody knew it: the guys on the field, the guys on the bench, everybody in the stadium. Layne would get the guy's number who creamed him, figure out whose fault it was, and call you right out of the huddle. He'd stand there raving at you and shaking a finger in your face and you wanted to punch him. One time he was chewing out Charley Ane so bad they almost had to pull him off Bobby. He was ready to go after him."

Baltimore Colts great Art Donovan recalled once watching Gino Marchetti, who Layne considered one of if not the best defensive linemen he ever faced, sneak past Creekmur and smash into Layne.

"I looked over at the huddle and there was Bobby kicking Creekmur in the shins. Lou just stood there and took it."

JERRY KRAMER: TRAINING CAMP

I went to jail today. I started an eight-week sentence in Sensenbrenner Hall, which is the student dormitory at St. Norbert College in De Pere, Wisconsin, a 10-minute drive from Lambeau Field in Green Bay. Eight weeks a year, since 1958, I've lived in this dormitory; I deserve an honorary degree from St. Norbert.

The whole thing is a pain in the ass. The worst part is that you're completely a captive of [coach Vince] Lombardi and of football. It's not like you put in two hours in the morning, two in the afternoon, and two in the evening. You're required to attend breakfast at 7:00 A.M., ride the bus over to the stadium, ride back in the bus, eat lunch, go over to the stadium and back again, dinner, meeting, curfew. If you're lucky, you get an hour and a half or two hours a day to do whatever you want.

DICK BUTKUS ON "MEAN" JOE GREENE

Our game against the Steelers at Wrigley Field on Sunday, November 9, 1969, would be our single victory that season. [Bears coach Jim] Dooley had instructed me and Mike Pyle, the offensive captain, to kick anyone out of the game who was not giving it his best effort. We beat them, 38–7.

Sometime in the third quarter after a kickoff play had ended, Andy Russell and I walked back to the line of scrimmage, and at some point along the visiting bench, Pittsburgh defensive tackle "Mean" Joe Greene approached us and started tossing insults at me.

Then he spit in my direction.

I can understand why Greene did what he did. Hell, I did the same sort of thing all the time. He was trying to provoke me, figuring that if I went at him the refs would toss me, which would give the Steelers a better chance of getting on the scoreboard. Another possible motivation for Greene's behavior was that he was a rookie trying to make his mark. I didn't even mind the spitting that much.

So I stopped, looked at Russell, smiled, and said, "What does this rookie think I'm gonna do? Start a fight and get kicked out?" Then I looked at Greene and said, "You asshole!"

> "I think I played with pain, and I think most guys played with pain because they were afraid to come off the field for fear someone would take their job."
>
> —MIKE DITKA

ART DONOVAN: THE EATING CONTEST

Though I may have been the biggest player on the Colts, I was far from the biggest eater. That was a title that belonged to either Gino Marchetti or Don Joyce, and one day we decided to do something about it. We were up in training camp at Western Maryland College, and after the coaches left, some of the older guys on the team had the cook make up about a hundred pieces of southern fried chicken.

We put up $100 apiece and sat Gino and Joyce down to an eating contest: who could eat more chicken. The cooks put out a beautiful meal: chicken, mashed potatoes, gravy, and peas. And I had money on Joyce, so I was really ticked off when I saw that Marchetti was just eating the chicken, while Joyce was eating the chicken, the mashed potatoes, gravy, vegetables, the works. "Goddamnit, Joyce, don't worry about the trimmings, just the chicken," I told him. So he stopped after two helpings and began concentrating on the bird.

Well, Marchetti ate 26 pieces of chicken. And when Joyce hit 25, we said, "Great, two more and we win."

But Joyce said, "Hold on, I'm still hungry." He ended up eating 38 pieces of chicken.

But the thing is, we hadn't let him drink anything until he beat Gino, on account of we didn't want his stomach to fill up. So when Joyce had his 27th piece of chicken, he said, "Man, I gotta wash this down."

There was a big pitcher of iced tea in front of him, so we said, "Here, have it."

With that, he took four pieces of saccharin out of his pocket and put them in the tea. Then he turned to us and said, "I'm watching my weight."

THOMAS "HOLLYWOOD" HENDERSON: SPEAKING OUT . . . AND OUT . . .

I started things off by telling the newspapers that [Terry] Bradshaw was so dumb he couldn't spell *cat* if you spotted him the *c* and the *a*.

I told them that I didn't like Steelers linebacker Jack Lambert, "'Cause he don't have no teeth."

As for Randy Grossman, who would be starting at tight end because their regular, Bennie Cunningham, had knee problems: "How much respect can you have for a backup tight end? I mean, he's the guy that comes in when everybody else is dead. He's the last hope."

They tried to make me say that the Steelers had no class, but I wouldn't because they did. They had won two Super Bowls already, and they were a good team. I just said ours was better. They were the Steel Curtain. I said I'd bring my acetylene torch to the Orange Bowl and cut them up.

Nobody before me had been such good Super Bowl copy.

CONRAD DOBLER: BAD DECISION

During another game against the Bears, I talked [Cardinals coach Don] Coryell into letting Bob Young, our left guard, and me play on the extra-point block team because we'd been watching the snap counts from the sidelines and we were fast off the ball and we just knew we could get in there for the block.

Looking back, I wish I had just kept my mouth shut.

After the snap, one of Chicago's offensive guards, Noah Jackson, dropped back his inside foot, leaving a big, beautiful gap to the kicker and holder. I took one look at that gap and, tasting a blocked kick, came charging through as fast as I could. And as I did, Jackson delivered an uppercut that took me right off my feet and put me flat on my back. Young wound up breaking his wrist on the same play.

As we came off the field, me holding my back and Bob holding his wrist, we looked at each other and said, "Well, that's enough time on defense for one career, don't you think?"

KEN STABLER: LEARNING FROM BLANDA

George Blanda played brilliantly at age 43. In one five-week stretch, Blanda won four games, tied another, and earned himself AFL-AFC Player of the Year honors. In a 7–7 tie with the Steelers, [Daryle] Lamonica went down, so George went in and threw three touchdown passes, and we won the game, 31–14. The next week, trailing the Chiefs 17–14, George kicked a 48-yard field goal to tie the game as time ran out. The next week he kicked a 52-yard field goal with three seconds on the clock to beat Cleveland 23–20. Then he beat the Broncos with a 20-yard touchdown pass with less than three minutes left to play. There were four seconds remaining in the game against the Chargers when George kicked a 16-yard field goal for the victory.

I learned a lot from Professor Blanda. We would stand together on the sideline and analyze the offense when Daryle was in. I'd watch Daryle's attack and tell George what I would've done. Then he would advise me, tell me whether he agreed with my plan or not and why. He kept pointing out that it was just as important knowing what *not* to do as knowing what to do.

BART STARR: AFTER SUPER BOWL II

At the postgame party, [coach Vince] Lombardi was smiling and couldn't help getting in a little jab at Max [McGee].

"McGee," he said, "I can't figure you out."

"How's that, Coach?"

"I've been coaching for eight years, and I've never seen anyone like you. You're a hell of a receiver, but you drive me nuts. You make a circus catch of a pass thrown three feet behind you, then you turn around and drop one that hits you right in the numbers."

Green Bay split end Max McGee (No. 85) takes Kansas City cornerback Willie Mitchell (No. 22) for a ride in Super Bowl I at the Coliseum in Los Angeles in January 1967. McGee, from Tulane, played for the Packers for 12 years (1954, 1957–1967), and this was surely one of his greatest days, catching seven passes for 138 yards and two touchdowns as the Pack demolished the Chiefs 35–10.

[McGee] paused for a moment, then put his arm around me and smiled. "Coach," he said, "it's easy to explain. I haven't had much practice catching ones thrown right to me."

"One thing I always wanted: to be able to play one game when I wasn't hurt . . . because I never played a game that my ankle or my shoulder or my knee or my back or my hand wasn't hurt. I always wondered if I could play a complete game without injuries, without that little edge of pain."

—L. C. GREENWOOD

DICK BUTKUS: STINKING CONDITIONS

Wrigley [Field] was originally a baseball field—a small baseball field at that—so small that wooden extensions had to be built over one of the dugouts to make room for the end zone. Then there was the locker room, barely big enough for a baseball team, only half what it should have been for a football team. Narrow wire-mesh lockers were jammed together, and rusting metal folding chairs competed for space. Hell, we even had it better back at CVS [the vocational high school Butkus attended in Chicago].

Cleanliness was a distant concept for the Chicago Bears. One time I smelled something awful and accused my teammate Doug Buffone of having rotten shoes, only to discover a dead rat behind my locker. But hey, that didn't matter to me because I was in the pros. And if this was how it was supposed to be, then it was just fine with me.

TERRY BRADSHAW ON ART ROONEY

I'd often visit him at his office. We'd puff on cigars until the air was blue with smoke. Sometimes I'd go into his office when he wasn't there, take the morning paper, help myself to one of his fat cigars, and sit there behind his desk smoking it. The first time I went in there and took a cigar, I left him a dollar. He kept that dollar until the day he died; to my knowledge it's still on his desk. I don't know how many times he caught me going through his cigar box. I felt like a kid with his hand in the cookie jar, but he told me to help myself. I could walk in there without saying a word to his secretary and have the run of the place. Usually I'd read his thoroughbred magazines.

Sometimes Mr. Rooney would walk in while I was there, pull up a chair, and sit on the other side of the desk. I always jumped up to move, but he'd insist I stay there. He'd say, "You look good in that chair! That's where you ought to be sitting! You're a big shot and I'm a nobody." He, of course, was as big a shot as the game ever knew.

ROCKY BLEIER: DIRTY TRICKS AT THE 1974 AFC CHAMPIONSHIP GAME

The Raiders had the best record in football. And they'd squashed us 17–0 in the third game of the year; we all remembered.

Oakland also has the reputation of being the "dirty tricks" capital of pro football. In previous years, they had slightly deflated the footballs our offense used, written obscenities on the balls, and smeared their linemen with grease so our guys couldn't hold them.

[Steelers coach Chuck] Noll was so paranoid about Raiders spies at our last practice in Oakland that he ordered us to run several plays from an unbalanced line.

If the Raiders' secret agents were watching, he reasoned, it would give them something to think about. Our game plan, of course, included nothing from an unbalanced line.

We ran everything else, though: dives, specials, traps, reverses. We even gained six yards on a busted play. Franco [Harris] rambled for 111 yards, and I—get this now—I ran for 98. Just 2 yards short of my first 100-yard game since high school. I wasn't even mad, though. How can you be mad after beating Oakland 24–13?

RAY NITSCHKE: A PACKER INSIGHT

Under [coach Vince] Lombardi, we never had any serious racial problems the way some other clubs had. We had some real fine blacks on the club, fellows who were real gentlemen—guys like Willie Davis and Willie Wood and Herb Adderley and others, not only fine players but fine people. If we had any racial problems, I didn't know about them.

The Packers were the first NFL team to have blacks and whites rooming together on the road. That attitude was one of the reasons for the team's success. The black players had some problems in their off hours, living in a small city like Green Bay where there weren't too many places they liked to go to relax. But they learned to accept this. And it was a two-way street. I think Green Bay learned a lot from the ballplayers about not judging people by their skin color.

"Even when I was little, I was big."

—WILLIAM "REFRIGERATOR" PERRY

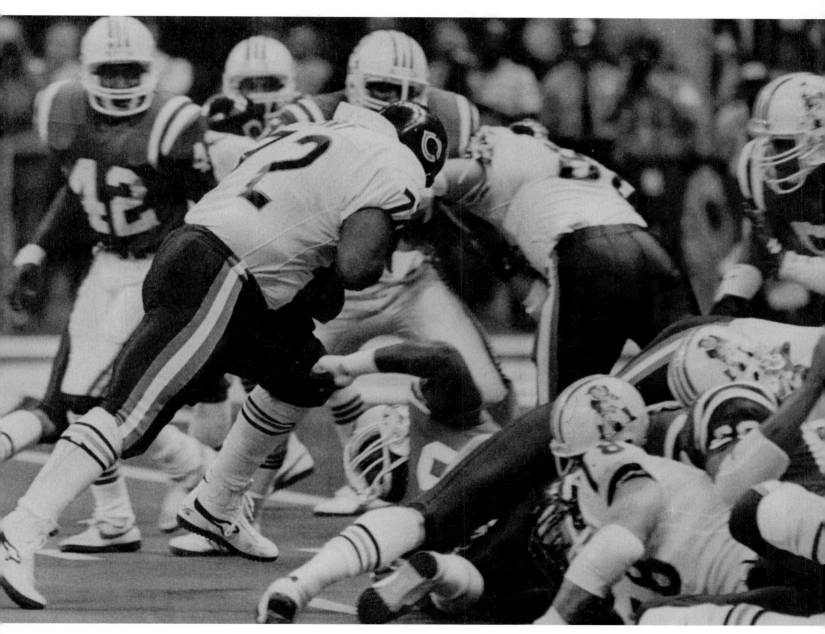

Defensive-tackle-turned-fullback on this play, William "Refrigerator" Perry (No. 72) plows in for a touchdown in Super Bowl XX at the Louisiana Superdome in New Orleans in January 1986. Perry, playing in the eighties when 300-pounders were a rarity, contributed most when he was on the defensive line for the world-champion Bears of 1985, but he proved to be more than a handful when he was converted to a ball carrier on special occasions. The Bears annihilated the New England Patriots that day, 46–10, then the largest margin of victory in Super Bowl history.

GEORGE BLANDA: A KICK TO REMEMBER

Once, when I was with the Chicago Bears, they sent me out to try a field goal against the Los Angeles Rams at the Coliseum in L.A. I line up and there's [Eugene] "Big Daddy" Lipscomb. He's a 6'8" tackle, and standing on his shoulders is Don Burroughs, a defensive back who is only 6'5". I'm supposed to get the ball over 13'1" of defensive players! The next year they outlawed all that.

LYLE ALZADO: THEY'RE TESTING ME

The Cowboys return the kick to their own 29. They try a reverse to their left side—[my] side—on their first play. Tom Landry is very big on opening the game with reverses. He opened Super Bowl X against the Steelers with a reverse to a linebacker on the kickoff, and the play made big yardage. [Butch] Johnson fumbles the handoff on the reverse, though, and Tommy Jackson smothers the play for a nine-yard loss.

Testing me. The bastards are testing me right away with a damn reverse. Can you believe that crap?

They challenged me, and I'm glad of it. Let 'em run at me all day. If they do, we're gonna win this game. [Ralph] Neely blocked down on me from the outside. I saw the handoff all the way: grip Neely on top of the shoulders, steer him, watch the tight end blocking down. OK, now hand-slide, let the tight end take his shot, then slide off it. I could spin, but Stan Jones doesn't want us spinning out this game. In the old days I'd have head-slapped the guy right off me. Head slap's illegal now. Damn! Anyway, I read the damn thing. I played it the way Stan wanted me to. Play the run first, then the pass.

Denver defensive end Lyle Alzado lunges for a scrambling Roger Staubach during Super Bowl XII at the Louisiana Superdome in New Orleans in January 1978. Staubach managed to evade most Broncos defenders that day as he led the Cowboys to a 27–10 victory and the NFL title; Staubach completed 17 of 25 passes for 183 yards and one touchdown. At this Super Bowl, Alzado was midway through his fine AFC career, which began in 1971 and ended in 1985.

MARCUS ALLEN: A LOSS HARD TO FORGET

Taking a handoff just inside the hash mark, I was headed toward the middle of the field when an Eagles lineman got his arms around my waist. Jerking in an attempt to free myself, I felt the ball slip from my grasp. Defender Seth Joyner somehow managed to bat the ball in the direction of his teammate, Andre Waters, who ran all the way to our 4-yard line before he was dragged down from behind by Dokie Williams.

[Eagles quarterback Randall] Cunningham scored two plays later.

The loss devastated me. Never before had I felt so singularly responsible for a defeat. Despite the efforts of several teammates who tried to assure me that there was enough blame for everyone, I sat in front of my locker replaying the horrifying moment of the fumble over and over in my head.

Finally, I looked up to see [Raiders owner] Al Davis standing over me, his face burning crimson, lips pursed. He just stared angrily at me for what seemed like an eternity before finally spitting out what was on my mind. "Aw, f***," he said. "I shoulda traded ya." And with that he turned and stormed away, never to speak kindly of me again.

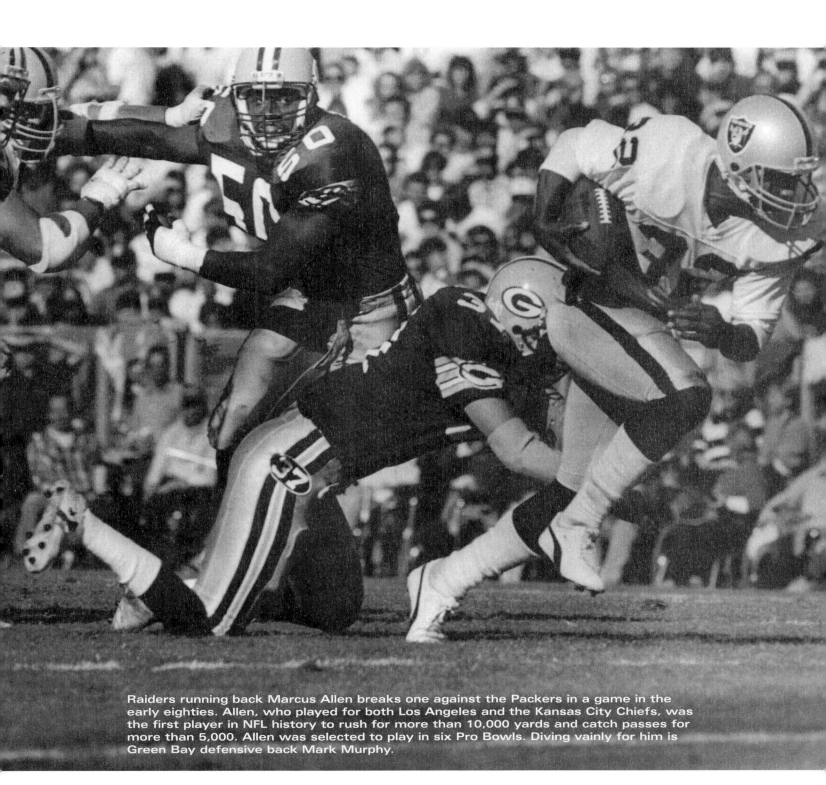

Raiders running back Marcus Allen breaks one against the Packers in a game in the early eighties. Allen, who played for both Los Angeles and the Kansas City Chiefs, was the first player in NFL history to rush for more than 10,000 yards and catch passes for more than 5,000. Allen was selected to play in six Pro Bowls. Diving vainly for him is Green Bay defensive back Mark Murphy.

Bibliography

Allen, Marcus, with Carlton Stowers. *Marcus: The Autobiography of Marcus Allen.* New York: St. Martin's Press, 1997.

Alzado, Lyle, with Paul Zimmerman. *Mile High: The Story of Lyle Alzado and the Amazing Denver Broncos.* New York: Berkeley Publishing Corp., 1978.

Bleier, Rocky, with Terry O'Neill. *Fighting Back.* New York: Stein and Day Publishers, 1975.

Bradshaw, Terry, with Buddy Martin. *Looking Deep.* Chicago: Contemporary Books, 1989.

Brown, Jim, with Steve Delsohn. *Out of Bounds.* New York: Zebra Books, 1989.

Butkus, Dick, with Pat Smith. *Butkus: Flesh and Blood.* New York: Doubleday, 1997.

Campbell, Earl, with John Ruane. *The Earl Campbell Story.* Toronto, Canada: ECW Press, 1999.

Delsohn, Steve. *Talking Irish: The Oral History of Notre Dame Football.* New York: Avon Books, 1998.

Ditka, Mike, with Don Pierson. *Ditka: An Autobiography.* Chicago: Bonus Books, 1986.

Dobler, Conrad, with Vic Carucci. *They Call Me Dirty.* New York: G. P. Putnam's Sons, 1988.

Donovan, Art, with Bob Drury. *Fatso: Football When Men Were Really Men.* New York: William Morrow and Co., Inc., 1987.

Dorsett, Tony, with Harvey Frommer. *Running Tough.* New York: Doubleday, 1989.

Flutie, Doug, with Perry Lefko. *Flutie.* Toronto, Canada: Warwick Publishing Inc., 1998.

Harris, Cliff, and Charlie Waters. *Tales from the Dallas Cowboys.* Champaign, Illinois: Sports Publishing LLC, 2003.

Henderson, Thomas "Hollywood," with Peter Knobler. *Out of Control: Confessions of an NFL Casualty.* New York: G. P. Putnam's Sons, 1987.

Jackson, Bo, with Dick Schaap. *Bo Knows Bo.* New York: Doubleday, 1990.

Karras, Alex, with Herb Gluck. *Even Big Guys Cry.* New York: Holt, Rinehart and Winston, 1977.

Klobuchar, Jim, and Fran Tarkenton. *Tarkenton.* New York: Harper & Row Publishers, 1976.

Kramer, Jerry. *Instant Replay.* New York: World Publishing Co., 1968.

Liebman, Glenn. *Sports Shorts.* Chicago: Contemporary Books, 1993.

Namath, Joe, with Dick Schaap. *I Can't Wait Until Tomorrow . . . 'Cause I Get Better Looking Every Day.* New York: Random House, 1969.

Nitschke, Ray, as told to Robert W. Wells. *Mean on Sunday: The Autobiography of Ray Nitschke.* New York: Doubleday, 1973.

Sahadi, Lou. *Steelers! Team of the Decade.* New York: Times Books, 1979.

St. John, Bob. *Heart of a Lion: The Wild and Wooly Life of Bobby Layne.* Dallas: Taylor Publishing Co., 1991.

Stabler, Ken, with Barry Stainback. *Snake.* New York: Doubleday, 1986.

Starr, Bart, with Murray Olderman. *Starr: My Life in Football.* New York: William Morrow, 1987.

Twombly, Wells. *Blanda: Alive and Kicking.* Los Angeles: Nash Publishing Co., 1972.

Whittingham, Richard. *Bears in Their Own Words.* Chicago: Contemporary Books, 1991.

———. *The Chicago Bears: An Illustrated History.* Chicago: Rand McNally, 1979.

———. *The Dallas Cowboys.* New York: Harper & Row, 1981.

———. *The Giants.* New York: Harper & Row, 1987.

———. *Giants in Their Own Words.* Chicago: Contemporary Books, 1992.

———. *Rites of Autumn: The Story of College Football.* New York: Free Press, 2001.

———. *The Washington Redskins.* New York: Simon & Schuster, 1990.

Index

233

234

243